English Grammar for Students of German

**The Study Guide
for Those Learning German**

Fourth edition

Cecile Zorach
Franklin and Marshall College

Charlotte Melin
University of Minnesota

The Olivia and Hill Press®

ENGLISH GRAMMAR series
Jacqueline Morton, editor

English Grammar for Students of French
English Grammar for Students of Spanish
English Grammar for Students of Italian
English Grammar for Students of Latin
English Grammar for Students of Russian
English Grammar for Students of Japanese
Gramática española para estudiantes de inglés

Library of Congress Card Number: 00-104926

Printed in the United States of America

ISBN: 0-934034-31-1

CONTENTS

CONTENTS

TO THE STUDENT

English Gramm;;'"ar for Students of German explains the terms that are in your textbook and shows how they relate to English grammar. This handbook compares English and German grammar, points out some of the similarities and differences between the two languages, and alerts you to common pitfalls. Once you understand your own language, it will be easier for you to work in German.

To save you time, we have examined frequently used German college textbooks and listed the topics covered in *English Grammar for Students of German* you should read. Just go to the web site: "www.oliviahill.com." Under "German" you will see a list of correlations that you can consult or download. If you are using a textbook not covered, check your assignment for the terms you need and find these in the detailed index of the handbook. When you finish a chapter in this handbook, you can test your comprehension by doing the short *Reviews* and checking your answers against the *Answer Key* (see p. 161).

─────────── TIPS FOR STUDYING A FOREIGN LANGUAGE ───────────

The goal of your German instruction is for you to be able to communicate with German speakers and to function in a German-speaking country. Learning vocabulary (words) and grammar (the way in which words are formed and combined) is an important part of developing your communication skills. The following suggestions will help you to become a more successful foreign language learner.

1. PRACTICE IN SEQUENCE—In your textbook, each chapter presents new material that depends on previously learned material. Make sure you understand each rule before you move on to the next one.

2. PRACTICE DAILY—Set aside a block of time each day for studying. Schedule short periods at different times during the week for listening to language tapes and working on computer exercises (if assigned). Always review your textbook before beginning assignments. Don't get behind. You need time to absorb the material and to develop the skills.

3. **LEARN NEW VOCABULARY**—Memorization plays an important role in language learning. One way to learn new vocabulary is by making flashcards. Write each vocabulary item on a separate index card with German on one side and English on the other. To review, look at the English word. Say the corresponding German word aloud or write it down; then flip the card over to check your answer. You can also use the vocabulary lists in your German textbook to learn new words. Look at the German words and say the corresponding English words. Then look at the English words and say or write the corresponding German words. Group related vocabulary items together (i.e., family members, hobbies, foods).

4. **LEARN NEW GRAMMAR FORMS**—You will need to memorize verb conjugations, noun and adjective endings, and other grammatical forms. Use index cards of different colors to help you remember useful information: the gender of nouns (i.e., blue for masculine, red for feminine, yellow for neuter), or the parts of speech (i.e., green for verbs, orange for adjectives, etc.). Use *English Grammar for Students of German* to compare grammatical structures and to learn how these structures function. This will make it easier for you to complete the exercises and activities in your textbook.

5. **TAKE NOTES**—Take notes in class. When your teacher gives you a new example or you hear a phrase while watching a video program, write it down so that you can analyze it. Once you have mastered a new concept, make up simple statements. Begin by modeling your sentences after the examples in your textbook. Later you will be able to express your own ideas.

Finally, we would like to thank Rebecca Raham, who provided updated materials for this edition of the handbook, and R. Blythe Inners for editorial assistance and preparation of the index.

"Viel Glück!"

Cecile Zorach, Charlotte Melin and Rebecca Raham

INTRODUCTION

When you learn a foreign language, in this case German, you must look at each word in three ways: MEANING, PART OF SPEECH, and FUNCTION.

MEANING

An English word may be matched with a German word that has a similar meaning.

Tree has the same meaning as the German word **Baum**.

Words with equivalent meanings are learned by memorizing vocabulary. Sometimes words are especially easy to learn because they are the same or very similar in both English and German.

GERMAN	ENGLISH
Haus	house
Garten	garden
Student	student
intelligent	intelligent

Occasionally knowing one German word will help you learn another.

Knowing that **Kellner** means *waiter* should help you learn that **Kellnerin** is *waitress;* or knowing that **wohnen** means *to live* and that **Zimmer** means room should help you learn that **Wohnzimmer** means *living room*.

Usually, however, there is little similarity between words and knowing one German word will not help you learn another. In general, you must memorize each vocabulary item separately.

Knowing that **Mann** means *man* will not help you learn that **Frau** means *woman*.

Even words that have the same basic meaning in English and German rarely have identical meanings in all situations.

The German word **Mann** generally has the same meaning as the English word *man*, but it can also mean *husband*. The German word **Frau** usually means *woman*, but it can also mean a married woman, *Mrs.*, or even *Ms.*

In addition, every language has its own phrases or way of expressing ideas; these are called IDIOMATIC EXPRESSIONS, or IDIOMS. For example, the word "keep" has a special meaning in the expression "keep your fingers crossed." You will have to be on the alert for these idioms because they cannot be translated word-for-word in German.

> In German the word **drücken** means *to press* and **Daumen** means *thumbs*. But **die Daumen drücken** means *to keep your fingers crossed* for good luck.

PART OF SPEECH

In English and German a word can be classified as belonging to one of eight categories called PARTS OF SPEECH:

noun	article
pronoun	adverb
verb	preposition
adjective	conjunction

Some parts of speech are further broken down according to type. Adjectives, for instance, can be descriptive, interrogative, demonstrative, or possessive. Each part of speech has its own rules for spelling, pronunciation and use.

In order to choose the correct German equivalent of an English word, you must learn to identify its part of speech. For example, look at the word *that* in the following sentences.

Have you read *that* newspaper?
adjective (see p. 107) → **diese**

She said *that* she was busy.
subordinating conjunction (see p. 133) → **dass**

Here is the record *that* he bought.
relative pronoun (see p. 137) → **die**

The English word is the same in all three sentences. In German, however, three different words are used, and three different sets of rules apply because each *that* belongs to a different part of speech.

FUNCTION

In English and German the role a word plays in a sentence is called its FUNCTION. Depending on the sentence, the same word can have a variety of functions:

subject
direct object

indirect object
object of a preposition   80

In order to choose the correct German equivalent of an English word, you must learn to identify its function. Let us look at the function of the word *her* in the following sentences.

I don't know *her.*
|
direct object (see p. 52) → **sie**

Have you told *her* your story?
|
indirect object (see p. 54) → **ihr**
                                                     90

The English word is the same in both sentences, but in German two different words will be used because each *her* has a different function.

───────────────── **SUMMARY** ─────────────────

As a student of German you must learn to recognize both the part of speech and the function of each word in a sentence. This is essential because words in a German sentence have a great deal of influence on one another. Compare the following sentence in English and in German.   100

The small blue book is on the big old table.

Das kleine blaue **Buch** ist auf dem großen alten Tisch.

In English, the only word that affects another word in the sentence is *book,* which causes us to say *is.* If the word were *books,* we would have to say *are.*

In German, the word for *book* (**Buch**) not only affects the word for *is* (**ist**), but also the spelling and pronunciation of the German words for *the* (**das**), *small* (**kleine**), and *blue* (**blaue**). The words for *is on* (**ist auf**) and *table* (**Tisch**)   110
affect the spelling and pronunciation of the equivalent words for *the* (**dem**), *big* (**großen**), and *old* (**alten**). The only word not affected by the words surrounding it is the word for *on* (**auf**).

Since parts of speech and function are usually determined in the same way in English and in German, this handbook will first show you how to identify them in English. You will then learn to compare English and German constructions, focusing on similarities and differ-   120
ences. This will give you a better understanding of the explanations in your German textbook.

CHAPTER

WHAT IS A NOUN?

A **NOUN** is a word that can be the name of a person, animal, place, thing, event, or idea.

- a person   friend, sister, student, gardener, doctor, Jacob, Katie, Professor Meyer
- an animal   dog, falcon, fish, bear, Snoopy, Fluffy, Mickey Mouse
- a place   stadium, restaurant, city, state, country, Zurich, Bavaria, New York, Austria, Europe
- a thing   desk, house, border, water, hand, Monday, White House, Volkswagen
- an event or activity   birth, graduation, jogging, growth, the Olympics, Thanksgiving
- an idea or concept   truth, poverty, peace, fear, beauty, time, humor, justice, hatred

As you can see, a noun is not only a word that names something that is tangible (i.e., something you can touch), such as *desk, restaurant*, or *White House*, it can also be the name of something that is abstract (i.e., that you cannot touch), such as *truth, peace,* and *humor.*

A noun that is the name of a specific person, place, or thing, etc. is called a **PROPER NOUN**. A noun that does not state the name of specific person, place, or thing, etc. is called a **COMMON NOUN**.

Katie is my friend.
  | |
proper   common
noun   noun

A noun that is made up of two or more words is called a **COMPOUND NOUN**. A compound noun can be composed of two common nouns such as *ice cream* or *comic strip*, or a proper noun, such as *Western Europe* or *North America.*

IN ENGLISH ————————————————————

Proper nouns always begin with a capital letter. All the nouns in the list above that are capitalized are proper nouns. Common nouns, however, do not begin with a capital letter, unless they are the first word of a sentence or question. All the nouns in the list above that are not capitalized are common nouns.

To help you learn to recognize nouns, look at the paragraph below where the nouns are in *italics*.

The *United States* imports many *items* from German-speaking *countries*. German *automobiles*, ranging from moderately priced *models* to elegant *cars*, have earned a *reputation* here for their excellent *performance*. *Germany* also supplies us with fine *tools, cameras,* and *electronics*. Many *Americans* value *watches* imported from *Switzerland*. Nearly everyone in our *country* appreciates the *taste* of Swiss *chocolate*.

IN GERMAN

Nouns are identified the same way as they are in English. In German, however, they are very easy to recognize since all nouns, proper and common, are capitalized, regardless of where they are in a sentence.

TERMS USED TO TALK ABOUT NOUNS

- GENDER—A noun has a gender; that is, it can be classified according to whether it is masculine, feminine, or neuter (see *What is Meant by Gender?*, p. 6).
- NUMBER—A noun has number; that is, it can be identified as being singular or plural (see *What is Meant by Number?*, p. 10).
- FUNCTION—A noun can have a variety of functions in a sentence; that is, it can be the subject of the sentence (see *What is a Subject?*, p. 36), a predicate noun (see *What is a Predicate Noun?*, p. 39) or an object (see *What are Objects?*, p. 52).
- CASE—In German, a noun can have a variety of forms depending on its function in the sentence (see *What is Meant by Case?*, p. 31).

— REVIEW —

Circle the nouns in the following sentences .

1. Katie asks her teacher many questions about Europe.

2. Mrs. Schneider answers her students with patience.

3. Curiosity is an important part of learning.

4. Katie and her classmates hear stories about Berlin, the capital of Germany.

5. The class tours an exhibit about German settlers.

CHAPTER

WHAT IS MEANT BY GENDER?

[1] GENDER in the grammatical sense means that a word can be classified as masculine, feminine, or neuter.

Did Jacob give Katie the book? Yes, *he* gave *it* to *her*.
masc. neuter fem.

Grammatical gender is not very important in English. However, it is at the very heart of the German language, where the gender of a word is often reflected not only in the way the word itself is spelled and pronounced, but also in the way all the words connected to it are spelled and pronounced.

More parts of speech indicate gender in German than in English.

ENGLISH	GERMAN
pronouns	nouns
possessive adjectives	pronouns
	adjectives
	articles

Since each part of speech follows its own rules to indicate gender, you will find gender discussed in the sections dealing with articles and with the various types of pronouns and adjectives. In this section we shall look at the gender of nouns only.

IN ENGLISH

Nouns themselves do not have gender, but sometimes their meaning indicates a gender based on the biological sex of the person or animal the noun represents. For example, when we replace a proper or common noun which refers to one man or woman, we use *he* for males and *she* for females.

- nouns referring to males indicate the MASCULINE gender

  Joe came home; *he* was happy; the dog was glad to see *him*.
  noun (male) masculine   masculine

- nouns referring to females indicate the FEMININE gender

  Kay came home; *she* was happy; the dog was glad to see *her*.
  noun (female) feminine   feminine

All the proper or common nouns that are not perceived as having a biological gender are considered NEUTER and are replaced by *it* when it refers to one thing, place, or idea.

> The city of Munich is lovely. I enjoyed visiting *it*.
> | |
>   noun   neuter

IN GERMAN

All nouns—common nouns and proper nouns—have a gender; they are masculine, feminine, or neuter. Do not confuse the grammatical terms "masculine" and "feminine" with the terms "male" and "female." Only a few German nouns have a grammatical gender tied to whether they refer to someone of the male or female sex; most nouns have a gender that must be memorized.

The gender of most German nouns cannot be explained or figured out. These nouns have a grammatical gender that is unrelated to biological gender. Here are some examples of English nouns classified under the gender of their German equivalent.

MASCULINE	FEMININE	NEUTER
table	lamp	window
heaven	hope	girl
tree	plant	bread
month	season	year
state	Switzerland	Germany
beginning	reality	topic

Textbooks and dictionaries usually indicate the gender of a noun with an *m.* for masculine, an *f.* for feminine, or *n.* for neuter. Sometimes the definite articles are used: **der** for masculine, **die** for feminine, or **das** for neuter (see *What are Articles?*, p. 13).

As you learn a new noun, you should always learn its gender because it will affect the form of the words related to it.

CAREFUL—A German noun will usually have different forms when it refers to the different sexes. For example, the noun "student" has two equivalents, a feminine form **Studentin** for females and a masculine form **Student** for males.

ENDINGS INDICATING GENDER

Gender can sometimes be determined by looking at the ending of the German noun. Here are some common endings you will want to notice:

MASCULINE ENDINGS

- nouns referring to male persons that end in **-er, -ist, -ling, -ent**:

der Physiker	*the physicist*
der Pianist	*the pianist*
der Jüngling	*the young man*
der Student	*the student*

- names of seasons (except **das Frühjahr,** *spring*), months, days, parts of days (except **die Nacht,** *night*), geographical directions, and weather phenomena:

der Sommer	*summer*
der Januar	*January*
der Montag	*Monday*
der Mittag	*noon*
der Wind	*the wind*
der West	*west*

- most nouns which end in **-ig, -or, -ismus**:

der Pfennig	*the penny*
der Doktor	*the doctor*
der Optimismus	*optimism*

FEMININE ENDINGS

- most two-syllable nouns which end in **-e** (some common exceptions are **der Name,** *the name,* **der Käse,** *the cheese,* **das Auge,** *the eye*):

die Lampe	*the lamp*
die Seife	*the soap*

- nouns referring to female persons which end in **-in**:

die Studentin	*the female student*
die Professorin	*the female Professor*

- nouns which end in **-ei, -ie, -heit, -keit, -schaft, -ung, -ion, -tät, -ur, -ik**:

die Bücherei	*library*
die Drogerie	*drugstore*
die Dummheit	*stupidity*
die Möglichkeit	*possibility*
die Freundschaft	*friendship*
die Prüfung	*test*
die Reaktion	*reaction*
die Universität	*university*
die Natur	*nature*
die Musik	*music*

NEUTER ENDINGS

- nouns ending in **-lein** or **-chen**:

das Fräu**lein**	*the young woman*
das Mäd**chen**	*the young girl*

- verb infinitives used as nouns (gerunds, see p. 90):

das Lesen	*reading*
das Singen	*singing*

130

CAREFUL—Do not rely on biological gender to indicate the grammatical gender of German nouns that can refer to either a male or a female. For instance, the grammatical gender of the nouns **Kind** *(child)* and **Baby** *(baby)* is always neuter, even though the person being referred to could be male or female.

— REVIEW —

By consulting the list above, determine the gender of the following German words: masculine (M.), feminine (F), or neuter (N).

1. Lehrer *(teacher)*   M   F   N

2. Brötchen *(bread roll)*   M   F   N

3. Freundin *(friend)*   M   F   N

4. Sonntag *(Sunday)*   M   F   N

5. Buchhandlung *(bookstore)*   M   F   N

CHAPTER

3

WHAT IS MEANT BY NUMBER?

1   NUMBER in the grammatical sense means that a word can be classified as singular or plural. When a word refers to one person or thing, it is said to be SINGULAR; when it refers to more than one, it is PLURAL.

one *book*   two *books*
| |
singular   plural

More parts of speech indicate number in German than in English, and there are also more spelling and pronunciation changes in German than in English.

10

ENGLISH	GERMAN
nouns	nouns
verbs	verbs
pronouns	pronouns
demonstrative adjectives	adjectives
	articles

Since each part of speech follows its own rules to indicate number, you will find number discussed in the sections dealing with articles, the various types of adjectives and pronouns, as well as in all sections on verbs and their
20   tenses. In this section we will look at number in nouns only.

IN ENGLISH ────────────────────────────

A singular noun is made plural in one of two ways:

1. A singular noun can add an *"-s"* or *"-es"*.

book   book*s*
kiss   kiss*es*

2. A singular noun can change its spelling.

30

man   m*en*
leaf   lea*ves*
child   child*ren*

Some nouns, called COLLECTIVE NOUNS, refer to a group of persons or things, but the noun itself is considered singular.

A soccer *team* has eleven players.
My *family* is well.

IN GERMAN

As in English, the plural form of a noun is often spelled differently from the singular. German plurals, however, are less predictable than English plurals; there are more endings and more internal spelling changes than in English. As you learn new nouns in German, you should memorize each noun's gender and its singular and plural forms. The following list shows you how endings are used in German plural forms:

- no ending (**umlaut** added when the stem vowel is **a**, **o**, **u** or **au**):

das Zimmer	die Zimmer	*room*	*rooms*
der Vater	die Väter	*father*	*fathers*
der Finger	die Finger	*finger*	*fingers*

- the ending **-n** or **-en** (feminine nouns with the ending **-in** add **-nen**)

das Auge	die Augen	*eye*	*eyes*
die Frau	die Frauen	*woman*	*women*
die Studentin	die Studentinnen	*female student*	
		female students	

- the ending **-e** (**umlaut** is sometimes added)

das Bein	die Beine	*leg*	*legs*
der Tisch	die Tische	*table*	*tables*
der Bart	die Bärte	*beard*	*beards*

- the ending **-er** (**umlaut** added when the stem vowel is **a**, **o**, **u**, or **au**)

das Buch	die Bücher	*book*	*books*
der Mann	die Männer	*man*	*men*

- the ending **-s** (added to foreign words or words ending in vowels other than **-e**)

die Party	die Partys	*party*	*parties*
das Auto	die Autos	*car*	*cars*

Notice that German often uses an **umlaut** (¨) to form plural nouns. This changes both the spelling of the word and its pronunciation.

— REVIEW —

I. Circle the English words that are in the plural.

1. pencils

2. suitcase

3. business

4. feet

5. group

II. Under the Plural column, circle the parts of the German word that indicate the plural form.

SINGULAR	PLURAL
1. Wort	Wörter
2. Stuhl	Stühle
3. Kind	Kinder
4. Studentin	Studentinnen
5. Auto	Autos

4

WHAT ARE ARTICLES?

An **ARTICLE** is a word placed before a noun to show whether 1
the noun refers to a specific person, animal, place,
thing, event, or idea, or whether the noun
refers to an unspecified person, thing, or idea.

> I saw *the* video you spoke about.
>
> a specific video
>
> I saw *a* video at school.
>
> an unspecified video

In English and in German, there are two types of articles, 10
definite articles and indefinite articles.

──────────────── **DEFINITE ARTICLES** ────────────────

IN ENGLISH

A **DEFINITE ARTICLE** is used before a noun when we are speaking about a particular person, place, animal, thing, event or idea. There is one definite article, ***the***.

> I read *the* book you recommended.
>
> a specific book
>
> I ate *the* apple from your garden. 20
>
> a specific apple

The definite article remains *the* when the noun that follows becomes plural.

> I read *the books* you recommended.
> I ate *the apples* from your garden.

IN GERMAN

As in English, a definite article is used before a noun when referring to a specific person, place, animal, thing, or idea.

> Ich aß **den Apfel** von deinem Garten. 30
> *I ate **the apple** from your garden.*

In German, the article works hand-in-hand with the noun to which it belongs in that it matches the noun's gender, number, and case. This "matching" is called **AGREEMENT** (one says that "the article *agrees* with the noun"). (See *What is Meant by Gender?*, p. 6; *What is Meant by Number?*, p. 10; and *What is Meant by Case?*, p. 31).

A different definite article is used, depending on three factors:

1. GENDER—whether the noun is masculine, feminine or neuter.
2. NUMBER—whether the noun is singular or plural
3. CASE—the function of the noun in the sentence

This chapter discusses only the basic form of the article as it is listed in the dictionary or in your textbook's vocabulary lists.

There are four forms of the definite article: three singular forms and one plural.

- **der** indicates that the noun is masculine singular
    der Baum   *the tree*

- **die** indicates that the noun is feminine singular
    die Tür   *the door*

- **das** indicates that the noun is neuter singular
    das Haus   *the house*

- **die** is also the plural of definite articles (masculine, feminine, and neuter)
    die Türen   *the doors*

Since the same definite article **die** is used with plural nouns and with feminine singular nouns, you will have to rely on other indicators to determine the number of the noun. The most common indicator is the form of the noun itself: is it the singular form or the plural form?

    die **Tür**
    the door
        Tür is a singular noun; therefore, **die** is feminine singular.

    die **Türen**
    the doors
        Türen is a plural noun; therefore, **die** is plural.

You will discover other indicators of number as you learn more German (see *What is a Verb Conjugation?*, p. 41).

──────────── **INDEFINITE ARTICLES** ────────────

IN ENGLISH

An indefinite article is used before a noun when we are speaking about an unspecified person, animal, place, thing, event, or idea. There are two indefinite articles, *a* and *an.*

- *a* is used before a word beginning with a consonant

    I saw *a* video at school.

    not a specific video

- *an* is used before a word beginning with a vowel

    I ate *an* apple.

    not a specific apple

The indefinite article is used only with a singular noun; it is dropped when the noun becomes plural. At times the word *some* is used to replace it, but it is usually omitted.

    I saw videos at school.
    I saw *(some)* videos at school.

    I ate apples.
    I ate *(some)* apples.

IN GERMAN

As in English, an indefinite article is used before a noun when we are not speaking about a specific person, animal, place, thing, event, or idea. As in English, the indefinite article is used only with a singular noun. Just as with German definite articles, indefinite articles must agree with the noun in gender, number, and case. There are two forms of the indefinite article.

- **ein** indicates that the noun is masculine or neuter

    ein Baum   *a tree*

    masculine

    ein Haus   *a house*

    neuter

- **eine** indicates that the noun is feminine

    eine Tür   *a door*

    feminine

Your textbook will instruct you on the different forms of the definite and indefinite articles in greater detail.

90

100

110

— *REVIEW* —

Below is a list of English nouns preceded by a definite or indefinite article.

- Write the corresponding German article for each noun on the line provided. The German dictionary entry indicates whether the noun is masculine (m.), feminine (f.), or neuter (n.).

	DICTIONARY ENTRY	GERMAN ARTICLE
1. the book	Buch, *n.*	_____
2. a table	Tisch, *m.*	_____
3. a class	Klasse, *f.*	_____
4. the telephone	Telefon, *n.*	_____
5. a car	Auto, *n.*	_____
6. the sister	Schwester, *f.*	_____
7. the ball	Ball, *m.*	_____

WHAT IS A PRONOUN?

A pronoun is a word used in place of one or more nouns. It [1]
may stand, therefore, for a person, place, thing, or idea.

> *Karen* likes to sing. *She* practices every day.
> | |
>   noun   pronoun

In the example above, the pronoun *she* refers to the proper noun *Karen* (see *What is a Noun?*, p. 4). A pronoun is
always used to refer to someone (or something) that has
already been mentioned. The word that the pronoun
replaces is called the ANTECEDENT of the pronoun. *Karen* is [10]
the antecedent of the pronoun *she*.

IN ENGLISH ———————————————————————————————

There are different types of pronouns, each serving a different function and following different rules. The list
below presents the most important types and refers you to
the section where they are discussed.

PERSONAL PRONOUNS—These pronouns refer to different
persons (i.e., *me, you, her)* and they change their form
according to the function they have in a sentence (see
p. 33). The personal pronouns include: [20]

SUBJECT PRONOUNS—These pronouns are used as the subject of a verb (see p. 37).
> *I* go.
> *They* read.
> *He* runs.

OBJECT PRONOUNS—These pronouns are used as:
- direct objects of a verb (see p. 58)
> Jane loves *him.*
> Mark saw *them* at the theater. [30]

- indirect objects of a verb (see p. 58)
> The boy wrote *me* the letter.
> Petra gave *us* the book.

- objects of a preposition (see p. 131)
> Angela is going to the movies with *us.*
> Don't step on it; walk around *it.*

REFLEXIVE PRONOUNS—These pronouns refer back to the subject of the sentence (see p. 120).

> I cut *myself.*
> She spoke about *herself.*

INTERROGATIVE PRONOUNS—These pronouns are used in questions (see p. 95).

> *Who* is that?
> *What* do you want?

POSSESSIVE PRONOUNS—These pronouns are used to show possession (see p. 101).

> *Whose* book is that? Mine.
> *Yours* is on the table.

RELATIVE PRONOUNS—These pronouns are used to introduce relative subordinate clauses (see p. 137).

> The man who came is very nice.
> Meg, whom you met, wants to study in Berlin.

IN GERMAN

Pronouns are identified in the same way as in English. The most important difference is that German pronouns have more forms than English pronouns since they must agree in gender, number and case with the nouns they replace (see *What is Meant by Gender?*, p. 6, *What is Meant by Number?*, p. 10, and *What is Meant by Case?*, p. 31).

— REVIEW —

Circle the pronouns in the sentences below.
- Draw an arrow from the pronoun to its antecedent(s).

1. Did Brooke phone? Yes, she called a few minutes ago.

2. Molly and Stan were out. They had a lot of errands to run.

3. If the paper is not next to the chair, look under it.

4. Jim baked the cake himself.

5. Has Brad met Helga yet? Yes, Brad already knows her.

WHAT IS A PERSONAL PRONOUN?

A **PERSONAL PRONOUN** is a word used to refer to a   1
person or thing that has previously been mentioned.

> Mike reads a book. *He* reads *it.*
> > *He* is a pronoun replacing a person, *Mike.*
> > *It* is a pronoun replacing a thing, *book.*

Personal pronouns can function as subjects, objects, and
objects of prepositions. These functions are discussed in
separate sections: *What is a Subject Pronoun?*, p. 37 and
What are Direct and Indirect Object Pronouns?, p. 58, and   10
What are Object of Preposition Pronouns?, p. 131.

In English and in German, personal pronouns, as well as
other parts of speech, are often referred to by the **PERSON**
to which they belong: 1st, 2nd, or 3rd, singular or plural. The
word "person" in this instance is a grammatical term
which does not necessarily mean a human being; it can
also mean a thing.

IN ENGLISH ──────────────────────────────

Each of the six "persons" is used to refer to one or more
persons or things. We have listed them in the order they   20
are usually presented and given the equivalent subject
pronoun. Sometimes, as in the case of the 3rd person, more
than one pronoun *(he, she,* and *it)* belongs to the same
person.

> **SINGULAR**
> > **1st PERSON PRONOUN**
> > > used by the person speaking   I
> > **2nd PERSON PRONOUN**
> > > used to address the person spoken to   you
> > **3rd PERSON PRONOUNS**   30
> > > used for the person or thing spoken about   he, she, it
> **PLURAL**
> > **1st PERSON PRONOUN**
> > > used by the persons speaking   we
> > **2nd PERSON PRONOUN**
> > > used to address the persons spoken to   you
> > **3rd PERSON PRONOUNS**
> > > used for the persons or things spoken about   they

As you can see, all the personal pronouns, except *you*, show whether one person or more than one is involved. For instance, the singular *I* is used by the person who is speaking to refer to himself or herself and the plural *we* is used by the person speaking to refer to himself or herself plus others.

IN GERMAN

German subject pronouns are also identified as 1ˢᵗ, 2ⁿᵈ, and 3ʳᵈ persons, each having a singular and a plural form. They are usually presented in the following order:

SINGULAR

1ˢᵗ PERSON	*I*	ich	
2ⁿᵈ PERSON	*you*	{ du	FAMILIAR
		Sie	FORMAL
3ᴿᴰ PERSON	{ *he*	{ er	MASCULINE
	she	sie	FEMININE
	it	es	NEUTER

PLURAL

1ˢᵗ PERSON	*we*	wir	
2ⁿᴰ PERSON	*you*	{ ihr	FAMILIAR
		Sie	FORMAL
3ᴿᴰ PERSON	*they*	sie	

CHOOSING THE CORRECT "PERSON"

Let us look at the English pronouns that have more than one equivalent in German: *you* and *it*.

"YOU"

IN ENGLISH

The same pronoun "you" is used to address one or more than one person.

> Mary, are *you* coming with me?
> Mary and Paul, are *you* coming with me?

The same pronoun "you" is used to address anyone (person or animal), regardless of their rank.

> Do *you* have any questions, Mr. President?
> *You* are a good dog, Heidi.

IN GERMAN

There are two sets of pronouns for *you,* the FAMILIAR FORM and the FORMAL FORM.

—— FAMILIAR "YOU" → DU OR IHR ——

The familiar forms of *you* are used to address members of one's family (notice that the word "familiar" is similar to the word "family"), persons you call by their first name, children and pets.

- to address one person (2ⁿᵈ person singular) → **du**

    Mary, are *you* there?

    du

    John, are *you* there?

    du

- to address more than one person (2ⁿᵈ person plural) to whom you would say **du** individually → **ihr**

    John and Peter, are *you* there?

    ihr

——— FORMAL "YOU" → SIE ———

The formal form of *you* is used to address persons you do not know well enough to call by their first name or to whom you should show respect (Ms. Smith, Mr. Jones, Dr. Anderson, Professor Schneider). There is only one form, **Sie**, regardless of whether you are addressing one or more persons.

    Professor Schneider, are *you* there?

    Sie

    Professor Schneider and Mrs. Schneider, are *you* there?

    Sie

Note that the formal *you* form **Sie** is always capitalized. It should help you distinguish it from **sie** the German pronoun for *she* and **sie** the German pronoun for *they*.

If in doubt as to whether to use the familiar or formal forms when addressing an adult, use the formal form. It shows respect for the person you are talking to and use of familiar forms might be considered rude.

——————— "IT" ———————

IN ENGLISH

Whenever you are speaking about one thing or idea, you use the personal pronoun *it*.

    Where is the pencil? *It* is lying on the table.
    John has an idea. *It* is very interesting.

IN GERMAN

The personal pronoun used depends on the gender of the German noun *it* replaces, its antecedent. Thus *it* can be either masculine, feminine, or neuter (see *What is Meant by Gender?*, p. 6).

To choose the correct form of *it*, you must identify two things:

     1. ANTECEDENT—Find the noun *it* replaces.

     2. GENDER—Determine the gender of the German word for the antecedent

Here is an example for each gender:

- masculine antecedent → **er**

     Where is the pencil? It is lying on the table.
     ANTECEDENT: the pencil
     GENDER: **Der Bleistift** *(pencil)* is masculine.
     Wo ist der Bleistift? **Er** liegt auf dem Tisch.
                             masculine

- feminine antecedent → **sie**

     How was the trip? It was nice.
     ANTECEDENT: the trip
     GENDER: **Die Reise** *(trip)* is feminine.
     Wie war die Reise? **Sie** war sehr schön.
                           feminine

- neuter antecedent → **es**

     Where is the book? It is on the table.
     ANTECEDENT: the book
     GENDER: **Das Buch** *(book)* is neuter.
     Wo ist das Buch? **Es** ist auf dem Tisch.
                      neuter

In both English and German personal pronouns have different forms to show their function in a sentence; these forms are called CASE FORMS (see *What is Meant by Case?*, p. 31).

WHAT IS A VERB?

A VERB is a word that indicates the action of the sentence.
The word "action" used in its broadest sense
is not necessarily physical action.

Let us look at different types of words that are verbs:

- a physical activity   to run, to hit, to talk, to walk
- a mental activity   to hope, to believe, to imagine, to dream, to think
- a condition   to be, to have, to seem

Many verbs, however, do not fall neatly into one of the above three categories. They are verbs nevertheless because they represent the "action" of the sentence.

The book *costs* only $5.00.
|
to cost

The students *seem* tired.
|
to seem

The verb is the most important word in a sentence. You cannot write a COMPLETE SENTENCE, that is, express a complete thought, without a verb.
It is important to identify verbs because the function of words in a sentence often depends on the word's relationship to the verb. For instance, the subject of a sentence is the word doing the action of the verb, and the object is the word receiving the action of the verb (see *What is a Subject?*, p. 36, and *What are Objects?*, p. 52).

IN ENGLISH ────────────────────────────

To help you learn to recognize verbs, look at the paragraph below where the verbs are in italics.

The three students *entered* the restaurant, *selected* a
table, *hung* up their coats and *sat* down. They *looked* at the menu and *asked* the waitress what she *recommended*. She *advised* the daily special, beef stew. It *was* not expensive. The service *was* slow, but the food *tasted* very good. Good cooking, they *decided, takes* time. They *ate* pastry for dessert and *finished* the meal with coffee.

IN GERMAN

Verbs are identified the same way as they are in English. Recognizing the difference between transitive and intransitive verbs, however, is more important in German than it is in English, because knowing whether or not a verb takes a direct object can help you identify parts of speech and determine the case of objects in German (see *What is Meant by Case?*, p. 31). You will find several examples of how verbs function differently in German and in English in the sections *What are Objects?*, p. 52 and *What are Reflexive Pronouns and Verbs?*, p. 119.

───────── TERMS TO TALK ABOUT VERBS ─────────

- INFINITIVE OR DICTIONARY FORM—The verb form that is the name of the verb is called an infinitive: *to eat, to sleep, to drink.* In the dictionary a verb is listed without the "to": *eat, sleep, drink* (see *What is the Infinitive?*, p. 26).

- CONJUGATION—A verb is conjugated or changes in form to agree with its subject: *I do, he does* (see *What is a Verb Conjugation?*, p. 41).

- TENSE—A verb indicates tense, that is, the time (present, past, or future) of the action: *I am, I was, I will be* (see *What is Meant by Tense?*, p. 69).

- MOOD—A verb shows mood, that is, the speaker's perception that what he or she is saying is fact, command, possibility, or wish, for example (see *What is Meant by Mood?*, p. 71).

- VOICE—A verb shows voice, that is, the relation between the subject and the action of the verb (see *What is Meant by Active and Passive Voice?*, p. 152).

- PARTICIPLE—A verb may be used to form a participle: *writing, written, singing, sung* (see *What is a Participle?*, p. 89).

- TRANSITIVE OR INTRANSITIVE—A verb can be classified as transitive or intransitive depending on whether or not the verb can take a direct object (see *What are Objects?*, p. 52).

— *REVIEW* —

Circle the verbs in the following sentences.

1. Katie and Jacob meet at the library.

2. The students eat their lunch at school.

3. We stayed home because we expected a phone call.

4. Rachel took a bath, finished her novel, and went to bed.

5. Sam felt better after he talked to his friends.

CHAPTER

WHAT IS AN INFINITIVE?

1   The infinitive is the verb form used to name
a specific verb. It is the form listed as the
entry in the dictionary.

The English-German dictionary lists *learn (v.)* **lernen**.

IN ENGLISH ─────────────────────────────────
In English, the infinitive is the dictionary form, that is,
the one-word form found in the dictionary (*speak, dream,
take*), as well as the two-word form, *to* + the dictionary
form of the verb (*to speak, to dream, to take*). In a sentence,
10   the infinitive is always used with the conjugated form of
another verb (see *What is a Verb Conjugation?*, p. 41).

To study is challenging.
infinitive conjugated verb

It *is* important *to be* on time.
conjugated verb infinitive

Bob and Mary *want to play* tennis.
conjugated verb infinitive

20   After verbs such as *must, let, should* and *can*, we use the
dictionary form of the verb without *to*.

Jackie *must do* her homework.
dictionary form

The parents *let* the children *open* the presents.
dictionary form

IN GERMAN ─────────────────────────────────
As in English, the infinitive is the dictionary form, that is,
30   the one-word form found in the dictionary (**arbeiten**,
work), as well as the two-word form, **zu** + the dictionary
form of the verb (**zu arbeiten**, *to work*). As in English, the
infinitive is always used with the conjugated form of
another verb.
The infinitive form always ends with the letters **-n** or **-
en**.

*Bob wants **to play** tennis.*
Bob will Tennis **spielen.**
   | |
conjugated verb   infinitive   40

*Mary doesn't have **to work.***
Mary braucht nicht zu **arbeiten.**
     | |
conjugated verb   infinitive

— REVIEW —

Write the infinitive form of the verbs in italics.

1. We *taught* them everything they know.   _____

2. I *am* tired today.   _____

3. They *had* a good time.   _____

4. She *leaves* next week for Konstanz.   _____

5. He *swam* every day in the summer.   _____

CHAPTER

9

WHAT ARE PREFIXES AND SUFFIXES?

¹

A PREFIX consists of one or more syllables added
to the beginning of a word to change
that word's meaning.

nuclear	→	*anti*nuclear
believe	→	*dis*believe

A SUFFIX consists of one or more syllables added
to the end of a word to change that word
into a different part of speech.

¹⁰

gentle (adjective)	→	gentle*ness* (noun)
love (noun)	→	love*able* (adjective)

To see how prefixes and suffixes work, look at the various
English words that come from the Latin verb **duco** *(to
lead).*

Different prefixes give us verbs such as *in*duce, *re*duce,
*se*duce, pro*duce,* and intro*duce.*

Added suffixes result in different parts of speech, for
example: induc*tion* (noun), induc*tive* (adjective), induc-
tively (adverb).

²⁰ **IN ENGLISH** ───────────────────────────

Most of our prefixes and suffixes come from Latin and
Greek. A good English dictionary will tell you the meanings and functions of the various prefixes and suffixes.

Knowing the meaning of prefixes can help you increase
your English vocabulary.

anti- + body (against)	→	*anti*body
sub- + marine (under)	→	*sub*marine
mal- + nutrition (bad)	→	*mal*nutrition

³⁰

Likewise, knowing English suffixes can help you identify
the parts of speech in a sentence.

-able, -ible	toler*able*	→	adjective
-ence, -ance	relia*nce*	→	noun
-or	debt*or*	→	noun

IN GERMAN

Prefixes and suffixes can communicate information not only about meaning and part of speech but also about noun gender. Let us look at two of the many ways they affect the verbs and nouns to which they can be attached.

VERBS FORMED WITH PREFIXES

Verb prefixes are quite versatile and function very differently from English prefixes. They are divided into two groups depending on whether or not they can be separated from the verb. We shall consider each type separately.

SEPARABLE PREFIXES—The most common separable prefixes in German are the following: **ab-, ein-, weiter-, an-, mit, zu-, auf-, nach-, zurück-, aus-, vor-**. When these units are not prefixes, they function as independent parts of speech (see p. 129).

Let us look at two examples to see how these prefixes can be separated from the verb.

INFINITIVE	SENTENCE
ausgehen	Hans und ich **gehen** morgen **aus.**
(to go out)	*Hans and I are **going out** tomorrow.*
ankommen	Der Zug **kam** spät **an.**
(to arrive)	*The train **arrived** late.*

INSEPARABLE PREFIXES—The most common inseparable prefixes in German are the following: **be-, ent-, ge-, zer-, emp-, er-, ver-**. They function more like verb prefixes in English because they are never separated from their stem verb. When you learn a new verb formed with a prefix, memorize whether the prefix is separable or not.

Wir **besuchen** unsere Tante.
We're visiting our aunt.

Sie **erzählte** uns eine Geschichte.
She told us a story.

Du **vergißt** immer dein Buch.
You always forget your book.

The addition of a separable or inseparable prefix to a verb has no effect on the conjugation of that verb. The strong and weak verbs include verbs with both types of prefixes (see p. 67). Your German textbook will explain the rules for using verbs with separable and inseparable prefixes in different sentence structures and tenses.

40

50

60

70

80

—————————— NOUNS FORMED WITH SUFFIXES ——————————

Certain suffixes not only affect the meaning of a noun but also determine the gender of the noun being formed (see *What is Meant by Gender?*, p. 6).

90

- **-chen** and **-lein** → new noun is neuter
  These suffixes show that the noun is a diminutive, i.e., something reduced in size.

NOUN		NEW NOUN	
das Brot	*bread*	das Brötchen	*roll, little bread*
der Brief	*letter*	das Brieflein	*small letter*
die Frau	*woman*	das Fräulein	*young woman*

- **-heit** and **-keit** → new noun is feminine
  These suffixes turn an adjective into a noun expressing an abstract quality.

ADJECTIVE		NEW NOUN	
schön	*beautiful*	die Schönheit	*beauty*
frei	*free*	die Freiheit	*freedom*
möglich	*possible*	die Möglichkeit	*possibility*

— *REVIEW* —

I. Underline the prefixes in the following words.

1. decode

2. enlarge

3. misunderstand

II. Underline the suffixes in the following words.

1. dependency

2. graceful

3. sleepless

WHAT IS MEANT BY CASE?

CASE in the grammatical sense means that different   1
forms of a word are used depending on
the word's function in the sentence.

I see Paul in class.

the person speaking
function: subject

Paul sees *me* in class.

the person speaking
function: object

10

In the sentences above, the person speaking is referred to
by the forms "I" and "me." Different forms of the 1st person pronoun are used because in each sentence the person
speaking has a different grammatical function. In the first
sentence, *I* is used because the person speaking is doing
the "seeing" and in the second sentence *me* is used
because the person speaking is the object of the "seeing."

More parts of speech are affected by case in German
than in English.

ENGLISH	GERMAN	
pronouns	nouns	20
	pronouns	
	adjectives	
	articles	

FUNCTION OF WORDS

The grammatical role of a word in a sentence is called its
FUNCTION. The function is often based on the word's relationship to the verb (see *What is a Verb?*, p. 23). Here is a
list of the various functions a word can have, with reference to the section in this handbook where each function   30
is studied in detail.

SUBJECT—A noun or pronoun which performs the action
of a verb (see *What is a Subject?*, p. 36 and *What is a Subject
Pronoun?*, p. 37).

PREDICATE NOUN—A noun that is linked to the subject by a
linking verb (see *What is a Predicate Noun?*, p. 39).

OBJECT—A noun or pronoun which is the receiver of the
action of a verb (see *What are Objects?*, p. 52). There are

different types of objects: DIRECT OBJECTS (see p. 52), INDI-
RECT OBJECTS (p. 54), and OBJECTS OF A PREPOSITION (see
p. 55).

To understand the meaning of a sentence, we must identify the function of the various words which make up the
sentence. In English, the function of a word is usually
indicated by where it is placed in a sentence. In German,
the function of a word is established by its case form.

Knowing how to analyze the function of words in an
English sentence will help you to establish which case is
required in the German sentence.

IN ENGLISH

English words usually do not change form to indicate different functions. For instance, the same form of the word
is used if it is the doer of the action (the subject) or the
receiver of the action (the object). The function of a word
in a sentence is indicated by where it is placed in the sentence.

We easily recognize the difference in meaning between
the following two sentences purely on the basis of word
order.

> *The student* gives *the professor* the essay.
>> Here the student is giving the essay and the professor is
>> receiving it.

> *The professor* gives *the student* the essay.
>> Here the professor is giving the essay and the student is
>> receiving it.

These two sentences show how we can change the function of nouns by changing their place in the sentence,
and consequently change the meaning of the sentence. As
we shall see below, that is not the case with English pronouns.

The only part of speech to indicate case in English is the
personal pronoun, whose function is indicated not only
by its place in a sentence, but also by its case (see *What is a
Personal Pronoun?*, p. 19). As you can see in the two examples below, it is not only word order but also the form,
i.e., the case, of the pronoun that gives the sentence
meaning:

> *I* know *them.*
> *They* know *me.*

We cannot say, *"I* know *they"* or *"They* know *I"* because the forms "they" and "I" can only be used to refer to the person doing the action. If you learn to recognize the different cases of pronouns in English, it will help you understand the German case system.

English pronouns have three cases:

1. The **NOMINATIVE CASE** is used when a pronoun is a subject or replaces a predicate nominative (see *What is a Subject?*, p. 36 and *What is a Predicate Noun?*, p. 39).

> *She* and *I* went to the movies.
> └──┬──┘
> subjects =
> nominative

> It was *he* who did the deed.
> │
> predicate =
> nominative

2. The **OBJECTIVE CASE** is used when a pronoun is an object (see *What are Objects?*, p. 52).

> *They* sent *us* a note.
> │   │
> subject =   object =
> nominative objective

> *We* asked about *them*.
> │   │
> subject =   object =
> nominative   objective

3. The **POSSESSIVE CASE** is used when a pronoun shows ownership (see *What is a Possessive Pronoun?*, p. 101).

> Is this book *yours*?
> │
> possessive

> Kit called her parents, but I wrote *mine* a letter.
> │
> possessive

IN GERMAN

Unlike English where only pronouns change form to indicate case, in German many parts of speech reflect the function of the word in the sentence. The case of a German word is sometimes reflected not only by a particular form of the word itself, but also by the form of the words that accompany it. We have limited the examples in this section to the case of nouns (see *What is a Noun?*, p. 4).

CASE OF GERMAN NOUNS

German has four different cases for nouns, and each case reflects a different function of the noun in a sentence.

1. The NOMINATIVE CASE—used for the subject of a sentence and for predicate nouns (see *What is a Subject?*, p. 36 and *What is a Predicate Noun?*, p. 39). This is the form of nouns listed in a vocabulary list or a dictionary.

2. The ACCUSATIVE CASE—used for most direct objects (see *What are Objects?*, p. 52).

3. The DATIVE CASE— used for indirect objects and for the direct object of a few verbs that you will have to memorize.

4. The GENITIVE CASE—used to show possession or close relation (see *What is the Possessive?*, p. 63).

The accusative, dative, and occasionally the genitive case are used with the objects of prepositions (see *What is a Preposition?*, p. 126).

Most nouns indicate their case by the endings given to their accompanying article. Each case has a singular and plural form (see *What is Meant by Number?*, p. 10). The complete set of case forms for any noun is called the noun's DECLENSION. When you have memorized these forms, you are able to "decline" that noun. Look at a set of declensions for the German nouns **der Apfel** *(apple)*, **die Tür** *(door)*, **das Kind** *(child)* and **die Bücher** *(books)*.

	SINGULAR			PLURAL
	MASCULINE	FEMININE	NEUTER	
NOMINATIVE	**der** Apfel	**die** Tür	**das** Kind	**die** Bücher
ACCUSATIVE	**den** Apfel	**die** Tür	**das** Kind	**die** Bücher
DATIVE	**dem** Apfel	**der** Tür	**dem** Kind	**den** Büchern
GENITIVE	**des** Apfels	**der** Tür	**des** Kindes	**der** Bücher

As you can see, case affects the form of the noun itself only in the dative plural and in the genitive singular of masculine and neuter nouns. For the other cases, it is the definite article that accompanies the noun which reflects the number, gender and function of the noun. This pattern applies to all nouns, with the exception of a small group called WEAK NOUNS, which have different forms to indicate case. Your textbook will explain the declension of this group of nouns.

When the nouns are in their proper case, words in the sentence can be moved around without changing the essential meaning of the sentence. Look at the many ways one sentence can be expressed in German.

170

> *The mother gives the child the apple.*
> **Die** Mutter gibt **dem** Kind **den** Apfel.
>
> nominative   dative   accusative
> the mother   gives   to the child   the apple
>
> **Den** Apfel gibt **die** Mutter **dem** Kind.
> **Dem** Kind gibt **die** Mutter **den** Apfel.

To choose the appropriate case for each noun in the German sentences above, you need to go through a series of steps:

180

1. GENDER—Identify the gender and number of each noun in the sentence.

> *mother* → **die Mutter**→ feminine singular
> *child* → **das Kind** → neuter singular
> *apple* → **der Apfel** → masculine singular

2. FUNCTION—Determine how each noun functions in the sentence.

> *mother* → subject
> *child* → indirect object
> *apple* → direct object

190

3. CASE—Determine what case in German corresponds to the function identified in step two.

> *mother* → subject   → nominative case
> *child* → indirect object → dative case
> *apple* → direct object → accusative case

4. SELECTION—Choose the proper form from the declension you have memorized.

200

> Die Mutter gibt dem Kind den Apfel.
>
> feminine   neuter   masculine
> singular   singular   singular
> nominative   dative   accusative

Your textbook will show you the different case forms for the definite and indefinite articles and explain how to use them. As you learn more German, you will discover other ways in which case affects the form of nouns, pronouns, and adjectives (see *What is an Adjective?*, p. 103).

CHAPTER

11

WHAT IS A SUBJECT?

¹ In a sentence the person or thing that performs the action of the verb is called the SUBJECT.

IN ENGLISH

To find the subject of a sentence, always look for the verb first; then ask, *who?* or *what?* before the verb (see *What is a Verb?*, p. 23). The answer will be the subject.

> Peter studies German.
> VERB: studies
> *Who* studies German? ANSWER: Peter.
> *Peter* is the subject.
> The subject is singular (see p. 10). It refers to one person.

> Did the packages come yesterday?
> VERB: come
> *What* came yesterday? ANSWER: packages.
> *Packages* is the subject.
> The subject is plural. It refers to more than one thing.

If a sentence has more than one verb, you have to find the subject of each verb.

> The boys were cooking while Mary set the table.
> *Boys* is the subject of *were.*
> (Note that the subject is plural.)
> *Mary* is the subject of *set.*
> (Note that the subject is singular.)

IN GERMAN

In German, it is particularly important that you recognize the subject of a sentence so that you can put it in the proper case (see *What is Meant by Case?*, p. 31). The subject of a German sentence is in the nominative case.

> **Das Kind** spielt allein.
> ***The child** plays alone.*
> *Who* plays? ANSWER: the child
> Child (**das Kind**) is the subject, therefore **das Kind** is in the nominative case.

CAREFUL—In English and in German it is very important to find the subject of each verb so that you can choose the form of the verb that goes with that subject (see *What is a Verb Conjugation?*, p. 41).

12

WHAT IS A SUBJECT PRONOUN?

Pronouns used as subjects are   1
called **SUBJECT PRONOUNS**.

They ran, but *I* walked.
Who ran? ANSWER: They.
They is the subject of the verb *ran*.

Who walked? ANSWER: I.
I is the subject of the verb *walked*.

IN ENGLISH ────────────────────────────────

Below is a list of English subject pronouns. For an explanation of the various "persons" see *What is a Personal*   10
Pronoun?, p. 19.

SINGULAR
  1ST PERSON   I
  2ND PERSON   you
  3RD PERSON   he, she, it
PLURAL
  1ST PERSON   we
  2ND PERSON   you
  3RD PERSON   they

                                                                 20
The above personal pronouns can only be used as subjects
of the verb. English uses another set of pronouns when
the pronoun is an object of the verb (see *What are Direct*
and Indirect Object Pronouns?, p. 58 and *What are Object of a*
Preposition Pronouns?, p. 131).

IN GERMAN ────────────────────────────────

The form of the pronoun used for the subject is called the
NOMINATIVE CASE. These pronouns are used whenever the
pronoun is the subject of a sentence or whenever the
nominative case is required in German.   30

	ENGLISH NOMINATIVE	GERMAN NOMINATIVE	
SINGULAR			
1ST PERSON	*I*	ich	
2ND PERSON	*you*	du	FAMILIAR
		Sie	FORMAL

40

3ʳᵈ PERSON			
	he	er	MASCULINE
	she	sie	FEMININE
	it	er	MASCULINE
		sie	FEMININE
		es	NEUTER

PLURAL

1ˢᵀ PERSON	*we*	wir	
2ᴺᴰ PERSON	*you*	ihr	FAMILIAR
		Sie	FORMAL
3ʳᵈ PERSON	*they*	sie	

— REVIEW —

Find the subjects in the sentences below.
- Next to Q, write the question you need to ask to find the subject of the sentences below.
- Next to A, write the answer to the question you just asked.
- Circle if the subject is singular (S) or plural (P).

1. I go to college in the fall.

   Q: _____

   A: _____   S   P

2. My bother and sister are still in high school.

   Q: _____

   A: _____   S   P

3. During the school year, they don't work.

   Q: _____

   A: _____   S   P

4. Unlike my siblings, I have to work all year long.

   Q: _____

   A: _____   S   P

WHAT IS A PREDICATE NOUN?

A PREDICATE NOUN is a noun connected to the subject   1
by a linking verb. A LINKING VERB is a verb
linking interchangeable elements together.

> Mary is my friend. [Mary = friend]
> subject | predicate noun
> linking verb

IN ENGLISH

The most common linking verbs in English are *to be* and
to become. The noun which follows the linking verb is not
an object because it does not receive the action of the   10
verb (see *What are Objects?*, p. 52); instead the linking
verbs acts as an equal sign and the noun that follows it is
interchangeable with the subject and is called a predicate noun.

> Jody *is* a good student.
> linking verb   predicate noun

> Subject, *Jody* = predicate noun, *student*
> Predicate noun, *student* = subject, *Jody*

> John became a teacher.   20
> linking verb predicate noun

> Subject, *John* = predicate noun, *teacher*
> Predicate noun, *teacher* = subject, *John*

IN GERMAN

The most common linking verbs are **sein** *(to be)*, **werden**
(to become), and **scheinen** *(to appear)*. As in English, the
noun following a linking verb is a predicate noun, not an
object. Predicate nouns are in the nominative case, the
same case as the subject.   30

> Maria ist meine **Freundin.**
> nom. linking   nom.
> case verb   case
> *Maria is a good friend.*

> Linking verb, **ist** (form of *to be*)
> Subject, **Maria** = predicate noun, **Freundin** *(friend)*
> Both **Maria** and **Freundin** are in the nominative case.

John wurde **Lehrer.**

| | | |
nom. linking nom.
case verb case

*John became a **teacher.***

Linking verb, **wurde** (form of *to become*)
Subject, **John** = predicate noun, **Lehrer** *(teacher)*
Both **John** and **Lehrer** are in the nominative case.

CAREFUL—It is important that you distinguish predicate nouns from objects so that you can put them in the nominative case. (see *What is Meant by Case?*, p. 31).

— REVIEW —

Circle the predicate noun in the following sentences.
- Draw an arrow from the predicate noun to the subject with which it is linked.

1. The letter was really good news.

2. Carol became a doctor.

3. They are tourists.

4. Dan became an accomplished musician.

5. The swimming pool is our favorite place in the summer.

WHAT IS A VERB CONJUGATION?

A **VERB CONJUGATION** is a list of the six possible forms of the   1
verb for a particular tense. For each tense, there is
one verb form for each of the six persons
used as the subject of the verb.

> I am
> you are
> he, she, it is
> we are
> you are
> they are

Different tenses have different verb forms, but the princi-   10
ple of conjugation remains the same. In this chapter all
our examples are in the present tense.

IN ENGLISH ─────────────────────────────────

The verb *to be* conjugated above is the English verb that
changes the most; it has three forms: *am, are,* and *is.* (In
conversation the initial vowel is often replaced by an
apostrophe: *I'm, you're, he's*). Other English verbs only
have two forms. Let us look at the verb *to sing.*

SINGULAR

1ST PERSON	I *sing*	20
2ND PERSON	you *sing*	
3RD PERSON	he *sings* she *sings* it *sings*	

PLURAL

1ST PERSON	we *sing*
2ND PERSON	you *sing*
3RD PERSON	they *sing*

Because English verbs change so little, it isn't necessary
to learn "to conjugate a verb;" that is, to list all its possible   30
forms. For most verbs, it is much simpler to say that the
verb adds an "-s" in the 3rd person singular.

IN GERMAN ─────────────────────────────────

Unlike English, German verb forms change from one person to another so that when you learn a new verb you
must also learn how to conjugate it. The conjugation of

all regular and many irregular verbs, however, does follow a predictable pattern.

In the conjugation of most regular and irregular German verbs, there are four forms that look like the infinitive of the verb: the 1st and 3rd persons plural and the 2nd person formal, singular and plural (for example, **singen**, below).

―――― CHOOSING THE CORRECT "PERSON" (see p. 20) ――――

(see p. 20)

In your textbook, the 2nd person formal forms will either be listed after the 2nd person familiar plural forms or after the 3rd person plural form, as they are in the conjugation of the verb **singen** *(to sing)* below.

SINGULAR

1ST PERSON	ich singe	*I sing*
2ND PERSON FAMILIAR	du singst	*you sing*
	er singt	*he, it sings*
3RD PERSON	sie singt	*she, it sings*
	es singt	*it sings*

PLURAL

1ST PERSON	wir singen	*we sing*
2ND PERSON FAMILIAR	ihr singt	*you sing*
3RD PERSON	sie singen	*they sing*
2ND PERSON FORMAL (sing. & pl.)	Sie singen	*you sing*

To choose the proper verb form, it is important to identify the person (1st, 2nd or 3rd) and the number (singular or plural) of the subject.

1ST PERSON SINGULAR—The subject is always **ich** *(I)*.

> **Ich** singe leise.
> *I sing softly.*

Notice that **ich** is not capitalized except when it is the first word of a sentence.

2ND PERSON SINGULAR —The subject is always **du** *(you)*.

> Molly, **du** singst gut.
> *Molly, **you** sing well.*

3RD PERSON SINGULAR—The subject can be expressed in one of three ways:

1. the 3rd person singular masculine pronoun **er** *(he* or *it)*, feminine pronoun **sie** *(she* or *it)*, and the neuter pronoun **es** *(it)*

> **Er** singt schön.
> *He sings beautifully.*

Sie singt schön.
She sings beautifully.

Es singt schön.
It sings beautifully.

2. a proper noun

Anna singt gut.
Anna sings well.

Der Fischer Chor singt gut.
The Fischer choir sings well.

> Since the proper noun could be replaced by one of the 3rd person singular pronouns, you must use the 3rd person singular form of the verb.

90

3. a singular common noun

Der Vogel singt.
The bird sings.

Die Geige singt.
The violin sings.

Das Kind singt.
The child sings.

100

> Since the common noun could be replaced by one of the 3rd person singular pronouns, you must use the 3rd person singular form of the verb.

1ST PERSON PLURAL—The subject can be expressed in one of two ways:

1. the 1st person plural pronoun **wir** *(we)*

Wir singen gut.
We sing well.

2. a multiple subject in which the speaker is included

110

Peter, Paul, Mary und ich singen gut.
wir

Peter, Paul, Mary and I sing well.

> Since the subject, *Peter, Paul, Mary and I,* could be replaced by the pronoun *we,* you must use the 1st person plural form of the verb.

2ND PERSON PLURAL FAMILIAR—The subject is always **ihr** *(you).*

Molly und Win, singt **ihr** auch?
Molly and Win, do you sing too?

120

> Since the subjects *Molly* and *Win* (whom you would address with the 2nd person familiar individually), could be replaced by the pronoun *you,* you must use the 2nd person plural informal form of the verb.

2ᴺᴰ PERSON FORMAL (SINGULAR AND PLURAL)—The subject is always **Sie** *(you)*.

Frau Smith, kommen **Sie** mit?
Mrs. Smith, are you coming along with us?

Herr und Frau Smith, kommen **Sie** mit?
Mr. and Mrs. Smith, are you coming along with us?

Since the subjects *Herr* and *Frau Smith* (whom you would address with the 2ⁿᵈ person formal individually or together) could be replaced by the pronoun *you,* you must use the 2ⁿᵈ person formal form of the verb.

3ᴿᴰ PERSON PLURAL—The subject can be expressed in one of three ways.

1. the 3ʳᵈ person plural pronoun **sie** *(they)*

Sie singen im Chor.
They sing in the choir.

2. a plural noun

Die Kinder **singen** im Chor.
sie form
The children sing in the choir.

Since the noun could be replaced by the 3ʳᵈ person plural pronoun, you must use the 3ʳᵈ person plural form of the verb.

3. two or more proper or common nouns

Paul und Mary **singen** ein Duett.
sie form
Paul and Mary sing a duet.

Die Gläser und Teller **sind** auf dem Tisch.
sie form
The glasses and plates are on the table.

Since the nouns could be replaced by the 3ʳᵈ person plural pronoun, you must use the 3ʳᵈ person plural form of the verb.

─────── **HOW TO CONJUGATE A VERB** ───────

A German verb is composed of two parts, a stem and an ending:

1. The **STEM** is the part of the verb left after dropping the final **-en** from the infinitive (or with a few verbs like **tun** and **ändern** by dropping the final **-n**) (see *What is an Infinitive?*, p. 26).

Infinitive	Stem
singen	sing-
machen	mach-
kommen	komm-

In regular verbs the stem remains the same throughout a conjugation in the present tense. However, in certain verbs called STEM-CHANGING VERBS, the stem vowel changes in the 2nd and 3rd person singular. Your textbook will identify which verbs are stem-changing verbs.

2. The ENDING is the part of the verb which is added to the stem and which corresponds to the grammatical person.

As an example of the steps to follow to conjugate a verb, let us look at the regular verb **machen** *(to make)*.

1. Find the verb stem by removing the infinitive ending.

   mach-

2. Add the ending that agrees with the subject.

SINGULAR

1ST PERSON		ich mache	*I make*
2ND PERSON FAMILIAR		du machst	*you make*
3RD PERSON	er macht	*he, it makes*
	sie macht	*she, it makes*
	es macht	*it makes*

PLURAL

1ST PERSON	wir machen	*we make*
2ND PERSON FAMILIAR	ihr macht	*you make*
3RD PERSON	sie machen	*they make*
2ND PERSON FORMAL (sing. & pl.)	Sie machen	*you make*

As irregular verbs are introduced in your textbook, either their entire conjugation or their principal parts will be given so that you will know how to conjugate them (see *What are the Principal Parts of a Verb?*, p. 66). Your textbook will also indicate whether or not they are stem-changing verbs. Be sure to memorize these forms, because many common verbs are irregular (**sein**, *to be;* **gehen**, *to go;* **werden**, *to become,* for example).

— *REVIEW* —

I. Draw a box around the stem of the German verbs in the infinitive form.

1. denken

2. rennen

3. arbeiten

4. wandern

5. reisen

II. Write the stem and conjugate the verb **gehen** *(to go)*.

STEM: _____

ich _____

du _____

er, sie, es _____

wir _____

ihr _____

sie, Sie _____

WHAT IS A SENTENCE?

A **SENTENCE** is a group of words that act together as a complete unit. Typically a sentence consists of at least a subject (see *What is a Subject?*, p. 36) and a verb (see *What is a Verb?*, p. 23).

The girls ran.
subject verb

They were eating.
subject verb

Depending on the verb, a sentence may also have direct and indirect objects (see *What are Objects?*, p. 52).

The boy threw the ball.
subject verb direct object

Maria threw her brother the ball.
subject verb indirect object direct object

In addition, a sentence may include other words giving additional information about the subject or the verb; these words are called **MODIFIERS**. There are various kinds of modifiers:

- adjective (see *What is an Adjective?*, p. 103)

I saw a *great* movie.
adjective

- adverb (see *What is an Adverb?*, p. 124)

Yesterday I saw a great movie.
adverb

- prepositional phrase; that is, a group of words that begins with a preposition (see *What is a Preposition?*, p. 126)

Yesterday *after work* I saw a great movie.
prepositional phrase modifying *saw*

- participial phrase; that is, a group of words that begin with a participle (see *What is a Participle?*, p. 89).

Attracted by the reviews, I saw a great movie yesterday.
participial phrase modifying *I*

- infinitive phrase; that is, a clause that begins with an infinitive (see *What is an Infinitive?*, p. 26).

> *To entertain* myself, I saw a movie.
>   └───────┬───────┘
>   infinitive phrase

It is important for you to learn to recognize the different types of sentences, clauses, modifiers, and phrases, since in German they affect the order in which words appear in a sentence.

─────────────── **SIMPLE SENTENCES** ───────────────

A CLAUSE is a group of words in a sentence that contains a subject and conjugated verb. A SIMPLE SENTENCE is a sentence consisting of only one clause.

IN ENGLISH

There is no set position for the verb in an English sentence or clause, but the subject almost always comes before the verb.

> We went to the concert.
> └──┬─┘ └┬─┘
> subject verb

A modifier can also come before the subject.

> *Yesterday* we went to a concert.
> └───┬───┘
>   adverb

> *After the party* we went to a concert.
> └────────┬────────┘
> prepositional phrase modifying *went*

IN GERMAN

In a simple sentence the conjugated verb always stands in second position.

> Wir **gingen** in ein Konzert.
> *we* ***went*** *to a concert*
> └─┬─┘ └──┬──┘
> subject verb
>   1   2

> Gestern **gingen** wir in ein Konzert.
> *yesterday* ***went*** *we to a concert*
> └───┬───┘ └──┬──┘ └┬─┘
>   adverb   verb subject
>   1   2

This does not mean that the verb is always the second word in the sentence, because some groups of words, such as prepositional phrases, together count as one position.

Nach der Party **gingen** wir in ein Konzert. 80
after the party   **went**   *we to a*   *concert*
prepositional   verb   subject
phrase   1   2

Notice that the subject of the sentence is forced to move to a position after the verb when there is a modifier. As you can see above, only in the first example is it possible to put the subject before the verb. In the other sentences where there is a modifier, the subject must follow the verb.

90

COMPOUND SENTENCES

A **COMPOUND SENTENCE** consists of two equal clauses joined by a coordinating conjunction (see *What is a Conjunction?*, p. 133). In both English and German the word order is the same as for any simple sentence.

IN ENGLISH

The position of the verb can vary in a simple sentence, though the subject usually comes before the verb.

clause 1   clause 2
We came home, *but* they stayed. 100
coordinating conjunction

clause 1   clause 2
Every evening John plays the piano *and* his sister sings.
coordinating conjunction

IN GERMAN

It is important that you know how to recognize a compound sentence because the verb is in the second position of each clause. The coordinating conjunction is just a link 110 between the two simple sentences and does not count as the first position.

Wir **sind** nach Hause gekommen, aber sie **sind** geblieben.
   1   2   1   2
We came home, but they stayed.

Jeden Abend **spielt** John Klavier und seine Schwester **singt**.
     1   2   1   2
*Every evening John **plays** the piano and his sister **sings**.*

COMPLEX SENTENCES
120

A **COMPLEX SENTENCE** is a sentence consisting of a main clause and one or more dependent clauses.

The MAIN CLAUSE, also called an INDEPENDENT CLAUSE, is a clause that could stand alone as a complete sentence.

The DEPENDENT CLAUSE, also called a SUBORDINATE CLAUSE, cannot stand alone as a complete sentence because it depends on the main clause for its full meaning.

dependent clause   main clause

Although it was raining, we took a walk.

130

> It makes sense to say "we took a walk" without the first clause in the sentence; therefore, it is the main clause. It does not make sense to say, "although it was raining" unless we add a conclusion; therefore, it is the dependent clause.

IN ENGLISH

Distinguishing a main clause from a dependent clause helps you to write complete sentences and avoid sentence fragments.

IN GERMAN

140

It is important for you to learn to distinguish between the main clause and the dependent clause in German, because each type of clause has its own word order rules.

MAIN CLAUSES—the word order depends on whether the main clause is at the beginning of the sentence or at the end.

- if the main clause is at the beginning of the sentence, that is before the dependent clause, the verb of the main clause remains in the same position as in the simple sentence; that is, the verb will be in second position in a German sentence.

150

main clause   dependent clause

Wir **machten** einen Spaziergang, obwohl es regnete.
    | |
    1   2

*We **took** a walk, although it was raining.*

- if the main clause is at the end of the sentence, that is after the dependent clause, the verb comes right after the dependent clause which functions as a single unit of meaning and counts as the first position.

160

dependent clause   main clause

Obwohl es regnete, **machten** wir einen Spaziergang.
    | |
    1   2

*Although it was raining, we **took** a walk.*

Dependent clauses—in clauses introduced by subordinating conjunctions and relative pronouns, the conjugated verb stands at the end, except in a few special constructions.

dependent clause   main clause

Obwohl es zu regnen **anfing,** machten wir einen Spaziergang.

*Although it **was beginning** to rain, we took a walk.*   170

Your German textbook will explain this structure in more detail.

— REVIEW —

I. Underline the phrases in these sentences.
- Identify whether the phrase is a prepositional phrase (PRP), participial phrase (PP), or an infinitive phrase (IP).

1. It is important to do your best.   PRP   PP   IP

2. Before the play we ate out.   PRP   PP   IP

3. Chris remembered the appointment
   at the last minute.   PRP   PP   IP

4. They wanted to start early.   PRP   PP   IP

5. Jane spent an hour organizing
   her room.   PRP   PP   IP

II. Box in the dependent clauses in these sentences.

1. While you were out, someone called.

2. Although we were tired, we had fun.

3. They said that they were ready.

4. Let us know if you want to go with us.

5. After the sun set, the park closed for the day.

III. Underline the verb in the main clause.
- Write "2" above this verb to indicate that it would be in second position in a German sentence.

1. Last night it snowed.

2. They really looked surprised.

3. With computers the work goes faster.

4. Tomorrow I have an appointment.

5. By the time we arrived, things were over.

CHAPTER

WHAT ARE OBJECTS?

¹ Objects are nouns or pronouns that are connected
to the action of the verb or to a preposition.

Paul *writes* a letter.
        | |
      verb   direct
               object

Paul *writes* his mother.
        | |
      verb   indirect
               object

The boy left *with* his father.
                  | |
            preposition   object of a
                          preposition

We will study the three types of objects separately: the direct
object, indirect object, and object of a preposition. Although
we have limited the examples in this section to noun objects,
the same procedure can be used to establish the function of
pronoun objects (see *What are Direct and Indirect Object
Pronouns?*, p. 58 and *What are Object of Preposition Pronouns?*,
p. 131).

────────────── **DIRECT OBJECT** ──────────────

IN ENGLISH

A direct object is a noun or pronoun that receives the
action of the verb directly, without a preposition between
the verb and the noun or pronoun. It answers the question *whom?* or *what?* asked after the verb.

John sees *Mary.*
John sees *whom?* Mary.
Mary is the direct object.

John writes *a letter.*
John writes *what?* A letter.
A letter is the direct object.

There are two types of verbs: transitive and intransitive.

A **TRANSITIVE VERB** is a verb that takes a direct object. It is
indicated by the abbreviation *v.t.* (verb transitive) in dictionaries.

The boy threw the ball.
transitive direct object

She lost her job.
transitive direct object

40

An **INTRANSITIVE VERB** is a verb that cannot take a direct object. It is indicated by the abbreviation *v.i.* (verb intransitive) in dictionaries.

Laura arrives today.
intransitive adverb

Brian is sleeping.
intransitive

50

Many verbs can be used both transitively, that is, with a direct object, and intransitively, without a direct object.

The students speak German.
transitive direct object

Actions speak louder than words.
intransitive adverbial phrase

CAREFUL—Some verbs that are transitive in English are intransitive in German, while other verbs that are intransitive in English are transitive in German.

60

IN GERMAN

As in English, a direct object is a noun or pronoun that receives the action of the verb directly. It answers the question **wen?** *(whom?)* or **was?** *(what?)* asked after the verb. Direct objects are expressed by the accusative case in German.

Paula liest **das Buch.**
Paula reads *what?* The book.
Das Buch is the direct object → accusative case
Paula reads the book.

70

A few verbs take dative case objects in German instead of accusative case objects. Here are two examples:

- **danken** *(to thank)*

Sie danken **dem Polizisten.**
They thank *whom?* The policeman (**dem Polizisten**).
Dem Polizisten is the direct object in the dative case.
They thank the policeman.

- **helfen***(to help)*

> **Wir helfen dir.**
>> We are helping whom? You (**dir**).
>> **Dir** is the direct object in the dative case.
>
> *We are helping you.*

Your German textbook will indicate the verbs that take objects in the dative case, and you will need to memorize them.

INDIRECT OBJECT

IN ENGLISH

An indirect object is a noun or pronoun that receives the action of the verb indirectly. It answers the question *to* or *for whom?* or *to* or *for what?* asked after the verb.

> John wrote *his brother.*
>> He wrote *to whom?* His brother.
>> *His brother* is the indirect object.

> John did *his brother* a favor.
>> He did a favor *for whom?* His brother.
>> *His brother* is the indirect object.

Sometimes the word *to* is included in the English sentence.

> John spoke *to Paul and Mary.*
>> John spoke *to whom?* To Paul and Mary.
>> *Paul* and *Mary* are two indirect objects.

IN GERMAN

As in English, an indirect object is a noun or pronoun that receives the action of the verb indirectly. It answers the question **wem?** *(to* or *for whom?)* or **was?** *(to* or *for what?)* asked after the verb. Indirect objects are expressed by the dative case in German.

> **Jeff schreibt seinem Bruder.**
>> Jeff writes *to whom?* His brother.
>> **Seinem Bruder** is the indirect object → dative case
>
> *Jeff writes **(to) his brother.***

> **Susan tat mir einen Gefallen.**
>> Susan did a favor *for whom?* Me.
>> **Mir** is the indirect object → dative case
>
> *Susan did **me** a favor.*

SENTENCES WITH A DIRECT AND AN INDIRECT OBJECT

A sentence may contain both a direct object and an indirect object, either as nouns or pronouns.

IN ENGLISH

When a sentence has both a direct and an indirect object, two word orders are possible, one without "to" preceding the indirect object and one with the preposition "to":

1. If the indirect object is not preceded by "to," the word order is as follows: subject (S) + verb (V) + indirect object (IO) + direct object (DO).

> John gave his sister a gift.   130
> | | | |
> S   V   IO   DO
>
> *Who* gave a gift? John.
> *John* is the subject.
>
> John gave *what?* A gift.
> *A gift* is the direct object.
>
> John gave a gift *to whom?* His sister.
> *His sister* is the indirect object.

2. If the indirect object is preceded by "to," the word order is as follows: subject + verb + direct object + *to* + indirect object.   140

> John gave a gift to his sister.
> | | | |
> S   V   DO   IO

The first structure without "to" is the most common. However, since there is no "to" preceding the indirect object *(sister),* it is more difficult to identify its function than in the second structure.

IN GERMAN

As in English, a sentence can have both an direct and an indirect object. Make sure that you establish the correct function in the German sentence so that you put the objects in their proper cases. Your textbook will show you how to place objects in a German sentence.   150

———————— **OBJECT OF A PREPOSITION** ————————

IN ENGLISH

An object of a preposition is a noun or pronoun that follows a preposition and is related to it. It answers the question *whom?* or *what?* asked after the preposition.   160

> Josh is leaving *without Maria.*
> Josh is leaving *without whom?* Without Maria.
> *Maria* is the object of the preposition *without.*

The baby eats *with a spoon.*
The baby eats *with what?* With a spoon.
A spoon is the object of the preposition *with.*

IN GERMAN

As in English, the object of a preposition is a noun or pronoun that follows a preposition and is related to it. It answers the question *"whom?"* (**wen/wem/wessen**) or *"what?"* (**was**) asked after the preposition. Unlike English, however, German prepositions have objects in particular cases, usually accusative or dative, and sometimes genitive. As you memorize prepositions, you will need to learn which case each preposition requires. Look at the examples of three different prepositions, each requiring a different case.

um diese Stadt
accusative with **um**
around this city

von solchen Büchern
dative with **von**
about such books

wegen des Sturmes
genitive with **wegen**
on account of the storm

CAREFUL—As a student of German you must watch out for the following pitfalls:

- an English verb that requires a preposition before its object may have an equivalent German verb that simply requires a direct object in the accusative.

  She is looking for her coat.
  She is looking *for what?*
  Her coat is the object of the preposition *for.*
  Sie sucht **ihren Mantel.**
  accusative
  suchen *(to look for)* takes a direct object

- the preposition that follows an English verb may be different from the preposition that follows the equivalent German verb.

  He is waiting for his friend.
  Er wartet **auf** seinen Freund.
  on

I am asking you for advice.
Ich bitte dich **um** Rat.
about

210

Your German textbook will introduce phrases like **warten auf** + accusative object *(to wait for)* and **bitten um** + accusative object *(to ask for)*. Make sure you learn the verb together with the preposition and its case so that you can use the entire pattern correctly. Remember that German has structures different from English and avoid the error of translating word-for-word from English into German.

— REVIEW —

Find the objects in the sentences below.
- Next to Q, write the question you need to ask to find the object.
- Next to A, write the answer to the question you just asked.
- Circle the kind of object(s) you found: direct object (DO), indirect object (IO), or object of a preposition (OP).

1. The computer lost my homework.

Q: _____   DO   IO   OP

A: _____

2. She sent her friend a postcard.

Q: _____   DO   IO   OP

A: _____

Q: _____   DO   IO   OP

A: _____

3. My parents paid for the books with a credit card.

Q: _____   DO   IO   OP

A: _____

Q: _____   DO   IO   OP

A: _____

CHAPTER

WHAT ARE DIRECT AND INDIRECT OBJECT PRONOUNS?

¹ Pronouns used as direct and indirect objects are called **OBJECT PRONOUNS.**

> Michael saw *us*.
> Michael saw *whom?* Us.
> *Us* is the direct object of *saw*.

> My parents wrote *me*.
> My parents wrote *to whom?* Me.
> *Me* is the indirect object of *wrote*.

¹⁰ The various functions of object pronouns are established in the same way as the function of object nouns (see *What are Objects?*, p. 52).

IN ENGLISH ───────────────────────────────

Most pronouns that function as objects in a sentence are different in form from the ones used as subjects. When pronouns are used as the direct object, indirect object, or object of a preposition in English they are said to be in the **OBJECTIVE CASE.**

Compare the nominative and objective cases of English ²⁰ pronouns:

	SUBJECT	OBJECT
SINGULAR		
1ST PERSON	I	me
2ND PERSON	you	you
3RD PERSON	he	him
	she	her
	it	it
PLURAL		
1ST PERSON	we	us
2ND PERSON	you	you
3RD PERSON	they	them

Here are a few examples showing you the use of subject and object pronouns:

> *He* and *I* work for the newspaper.
> └──┬──┘
> subjects
> nominative case

The politician invited *him* and *me* to lunch.

                              direct objects
                              objective case

They took their car to the garage.

subject
nominative case

I lent *them* my car.

        indirect object
        objective case

You and *she* are going now.

subjects
nominative case

I want to go with *you* and *her*.

              objects of a preposition
              objective case

The form of the object pronoun is the same regardless of whether the pronoun is used as a direct object, an indirect object, or an object of a preposition.

IN GERMAN ——————————————————————————

Unlike English which has only one objective case for pronouns that are direct objects and indirect objects, German uses two cases, the accusative and the dative. Look at the chart below.

ENGLISH		GERMAN		
OBJECTIVE		ACCUSATIVE	DATIVE	
SINGULAR				
1ST PERSON	*me*	mich	mir	
2ND PERSON	*you*	dich	dir	FAMILIAR
		Sie	Ihnen	FORMAL
	him	ihn	ihm	MASCULINE
3RD PERSON	*her*	sie	ihr	FEMININE
	it	es	ihm	NEUTER
PLURAL				
1ST PERSON	*us*	uns	uns	
2ND PERSON	*you*	euch	euch	FAMILIAR
		Sie	Ihnen	FORMAL
3RD PERSON	*them*	sie	ihnen	

Two English object pronouns have more than one equivalent in German: *you* and *it*. Let us look more closely at these object pronouns.

──────────── **FAMILIAR "YOU" AS OBJECT PRONOUN** ────────────
(see p. 21 in *What is a Personal Pronoun?*)

The familiar forms of "you" can be singular or plural, depending on whether the "you" addressed is one or more persons, each form having an accusative and dative form.

SINGULAR—You are speaking to one person → **dich** (accusative); **dir** (dative)

> *We see you, **Anna**.*
> Wir sehen **dich**, Anna.
>
> sehen *(to see)* takes an accusative object

> *We are helping **you**, Anna.*
> Wir helfen **dir**, Anna.
>
> helfen *(to help)* takes a dative object

PLURAL—You are speaking to more than one person → **euch** (accusative and dative)

> *We see **you**, Effi and Franz.*
> Wir sehen **euch**, Effi und Franz.
>
> sehen *(to see)* takes an accusative object

> *We are helping **you**, Effi and Franz.*
> Wir helfen **euch**, Effi und Franz.
>
> helfen *(to help)* takes a dative object

──────────── **FORMAL "YOU" AS OBJECT PRONOUN** ────────────
(see p. 21 in *What is a Personal Pronoun?*)

The formal form of "you" has two forms, the accusative and the dative; the same form is used for the singular and the plural.

ACCUSATIVE—You are speaking to one or more persons → **Sie** (accusative singular and plural)

> *We will see **you** tomorrow, Mrs. Erb.*
> Wir sehen **Sie** morgen, Frau Erb.
>
> sehen *(to see)* takes an accusative object

DATIVE—You are speaking to one or more persons → **Ihnen** (dative singular and plural)

> *We are glad to help **you**, Dr. Fried.*
> Wir helfen **Ihnen** gern, Dr. Fried.
>
> helfen *(to help)* takes a dative object

──────────── **"IT" AS AN OBJECT PRONOUN** ────────────

Like English, German uses personal pronouns in the objective case to refer to people, **ihn, ihm** *(him)* and **sie, ihr** *(her)*. But where English uses one pronoun for "it," German has six different object pronouns depending on the gender of the antecedent (masculine, feminine, and neuter) and the case of the pronoun, accusative or dative.

To choose the correct form, follow these steps:

1. ANTECEDENT: Find the noun *"it"* replaces.
2. GENDER: Determine the gender of the German antecedent.
3. FUNCTION: Determine the function of "it" in the sentence.
4. CASE: Choose the case that corresponds to the function.
5. SELECTION: Select the form depending on the gender and case.

Let us look at some examples.

- if the antecedent is masculine → **ihn** (accusative) or **ihm** (dative)

    *Did you see the film? Yes, I saw **it**.*
    ANTECEDENT: the film
    GENDER: **der Film** *(the film)* is masculine
    FUNCTION: direct object of *see* (**sehen**)
    CASE: accusative
    SELECTION: masculine accusative → **ihn**
    Hast du den Film gesehen? Ja, ich habe **ihn** gesehen.

- if the antecedent is feminine → **sie** (accusative) or **ihr** (dative)

    *Are you reading the newspaper? Yes, I am reading **it**.*
    ANTECEDENT: the newspaper
    GENDER: **die Zeitung** *(the newspaper)* is feminine
    FUNCTION: direct object of *read* (**lesen**)
    CASE: accusative
    SELECTION: feminine accusative → **sie**
    Lesen Sie die Zeitung? Ja, ich lese **sie**.

- if the antecedent is neuter → **es** (accusative) or **ihm** (dative)

    *Do you understand the book? Yes, I understand **it**.*
    ANTECEDENT: the book
    GENDER: **das Buch** *(the book)* is neuter
    FUNCTION: direct object of *understand* (**verstehen**)
    CASE: accusative
    SELECTION: neuter accusative → **es**
    Verstehen Sie das Buch? Ja, ich verstehe **es**.

130

140

150

160

CAREFUL—In English you can only use the objective pronouns *him* or *her* to refer to people. In German, however, when you replace neuter nouns that refer to people you will have to use the neuter pronouns **es** and **ihm.**

170

> *Who helps the child? We are helping **her** (or **him**).*
>> ANTECEDENT: the child
>> GENDER: **das Kind** *(the child)* is neuter
>> FUNCTION: object of *help* (**helfen** takes a dative object)
>> CASE: dative
>> SELECTION: neuter dative → **ihm**
>
> Wer hilft dem Kind? Wir helfen **ihm.**
>> dative object

— R E V I E W —

Using the chart on p. 59, indicate the information requested about the pronouns in bold.

1. I believe **you.**

PERSON:	1st	2nd	3rd
NUMBER:	singular	plural	

2. We saw **him** often.

PERSON:	1st	2nd	3rd
GENDER:	masculine	feminine	neuter
NUMBER:	singular	plural	

3. They called **her.**

PERSON:	1st	2nd	3rd
GENDER:	masculine	feminine	neuter
NUMBER:	singular	plural	

WHAT IS THE POSSESSIVE?

The **POSSESSIVE** is used to show that one noun *possesses* or owns another noun.

Katie's German book is on the table.

noun — possessor
noun — possessed

IN ENGLISH

There are two constructions to show possession:
1. An apostrophe can be used. In this construction, the possessor comes before the possessed.
   - a singular possessor adds an apostrophe + "s"
        Inge's mother
        the professor's book
        singular possessor
   - a plural possessor ending with "s" adds an apostrophe after the "s"
        the girls' father
        the boys' school
        plural possessor
   - a plural possessor not ending with "s" adds an apostrophe + "s"
        the children's playground
        the women's role
        plural possessor
2. The word *of* can be used. In this structure, the possessed comes before the possessor.
   - a singular or plural possessor is preceded by *of the* or *of a*
        the book *of the* professor
        the branches *of a* tree
        singular possessor

        the teacher of the students
        plural possessor

- a proper noun possessor is preceded by *of*

> the poetry of Goethe
> |
>   proper noun possessor

IN GERMAN

There are also two ways to show possession: the genitive case is used in writing and in formal language and **von +** the dative is used in spoken German.

1. GENITIVE CASE—When the genitive case of a noun is used to show possession, the order in which the noun possessor and the noun possessed appear is different depending on whether the noun possessor is a proper or a common noun.

- a proper noun possessor—This German structure parallels the English structure that uses the apostrophe to show possession. Just as in English, the noun possessor, in this case a proper noun, comes before the noun possessed.

> **Inges** Mutter
> *Inge's mother*
> | |
> possessor possessed

In German the only time that an apostrophe is used for the genitive is when a proper noun ends in -s or -z.

> **Kiwus'** Gedichte
> *Kiwus's poems*
> | |
> possessor possessed

- a common noun possessor—This German structure parallels the English structure that uses *of the.* Just as in English, the noun possessor, in this case a common noun, generally follows the noun possessed.

Most masculine and neuter singular nouns of one syllable → add **-es**. Masculine and neuter singular nouns of more than one syllable → add **-s**. The accompanying articles also end in **-s**.

> der Ball des Kindes
> | | |
> possessed | possessor
> *ball* | *child*
> | neuter singular
> | one syllable **Kind**
>   genitive
>   definite article

*the ball **of the** child*
the child's ball

- feminine singular and plural nouns → add **-er** to the preceding article or adjectives. The noun itself has no special ending.

  der Mantel der Frau

possessed	possessor
coat	woman
feminine	singular

  genitive
  definite article

*the coat **of the** woman*
the woman's coat

Your German textbook will explain the genitive in greater detail and will point out the few irregularities.

2. **VON + DATIVE**—When the construction **von** + dative case is used to show possession, the same construction is used for proper and common noun possessor. The order in which the noun possessor and the noun possessed appear corresponds to the construction *of* + noun possessor in English.

  der Vater **von den** Mädchen

  von + dative

*the father **of the** girls*

die Mutter **von** Inge
*the mother **of** Inge*

— REVIEW —

The following are possessive constructions using the apostrophe.
- Write the alternate English structure using the word **of**.
- Underline the possessor in your new construction.

1. the cars' motor

_____

2. the year's end

_____

3. Bachmann's works

_____

4. the street's name

_____

5. Berlin's museums

_____

90

100

CHAPTER

WHAT ARE THE PRINCIPAL PARTS
OF A VERB?

¹ The principal parts of a verb are the forms we need
to create all the different tenses

PRESENT	I eat
PRESENT PERFECT	I have eaten
PAST	I ate
PAST PERFECT	I had eaten
FUTURE	I will eat
FUTURE PERFECT	I will have eaten

IN ENGLISH ────────────────────────────────

The principal parts of an English verb are the infinitive
(eat), the past tense *(ate),* and the past participle *(eaten).* If
you know these parts, you can form all the other tenses of
a verb (see *What is Meant by Tense?,* p. 69, *What is the Past
Tense?,* p. 81, and *What is a Participle?,* p. 89).

English verbs fall into two categories depending on how
they form their principal parts:

1. REGULAR VERBS—These verbs are called regular because
   their past tense and past participle forms follow the predictable pattern of adding *-ed, -d,* or *-t* to the infinitive.

INFINITIVE	PAST TENSE	PAST PARTICIPLE
to walk	walk*ed*	walk*ed*
to seem	seem*ed*	seem*ed*
to burn	burn*ed* (burn*t*)	burn*ed* (burn*t*)

Since the past tense and the past participle of regular
verbs are identical, regular verbs have only two distinct
principal parts, the infinitive and the past.

2. IRREGULAR VERBS—These verbs are called irregular because
   their principal parts do not follow a regular pattern:

INFINITIVE	PAST TENSE	PAST PARTICIPLE
to sing	sang	sung
to draw	drew	drawn
to hit	hit	hit
to lie	lay	lain
to ride	rode	ridden

IN GERMAN

Three of the principal parts are the same as in English: the infinitive, the past tense, and the past participle. For the past tense, the principal part is given in the 3rd person singular. German adds a fourth principal part for irregular verbs with stem vowel change in the 2nd and 3rd person singular of the present tense. This form is also given in the 3rd person singular.

to eat	essen	INFINITIVE
eats	isst	PRESENT TENSE (3rd person sing.)
ate	aß	PAST TENSE (3rd person sing.)
eaten	gegessen	PAST PARTICIPLE

German verbs fall into two categories depending on how they form their principal parts: weak verbs and strong verbs. A few irregular verbs fall between these two categories. Your German textbook will show you how to form the principal parts of these verbs.

WEAK VERBS

Weak verbs resemble English regular verbs in that the stem of the verb stays the same, despite other modifications to form the principal parts.

STEM—The stem is obtained by dropping the final -en from the infinitive (or with a few verbs like **tun** and **ändern** by dropping the final -n).

MODIFICATIONS—The various principal parts are formed by adding various prefixes and or suffixes to the stem.

- the past tense is formed by adding a -t- (or if the verb stem ends in -d or -t, by adding -et) to the stem of the infinitive and then adding the endings for the different persons.
- the past participle is formed by adding the prefix ge- and the suffix -t or -et to the stem of the verb. Note that a few weak verbs have past participles without the ge- prefix.

	INFINITIVE	PAST TENSE (3rd per. sing.)	PAST PARTICIPLE
to make	machen	machte	gemacht
to work	arbeiten	arbeitete	gearbeitet
to believe	glauben	glaubte	geglaubt

─────────────── **STRONG VERBS** ───────────────

Strong verbs resemble English irregular verbs in that they have unpredictable principal parts. You will have to memorize these parts as you learn new verbs.

The irregularity of strong verbs is shown in a variety of ways:

- the vowel of the verb stem will often change in the past tense and in the past participle.

- the past tense endings are different than those for weak verbs

- the past participle is usually formed by adding the prefix **ge-**, and it does not end in **-t** but rather in **-en** or **-n**.

	INFINITIVE	PAST TENSE	PAST PARTICIPLE
to find	finden	fand	gefunden
to come	kommen	kam	gekommen
to lose	verlieren	verlor	verloren
to sing	singen	sang	gesungen
to do	tun	tat	getan

- when the stem vowel changes in the 2nd and 3rd person singular of the present tense, you will need to know a fourth principal part, the 3rd person singular of the present tense.

	INFINITIVE	PRESENT	PAST TENSE	PAST PARTICIPLE
to run	laufen	läuft	lief	gelaufen
to read	lesen	liest	las	gelesen
to sleep	schlafen	schläft	schlief	geschlafen
to take	nehmen	nimmt	nahm	genommen

Only by memorizing the principal parts of the strong verbs can you conjugate them properly in all their tenses.

── *REVIEW* ──

Indicate whether the following German verbs are weak (w: end with -(e)t) or strong (s: end with -(e)n).

1. kaufen	kaufte-	gekauft		w	s
2. beginnen	begann-	begonnen		w	s
3. liegen	lag-	gelegen		w	s
4. fragen	fragte-	gefragt		w	s
5. sitzen	saß-	gesessen		w	s

WHAT IS MEANT BY TENSE?

The TENSE of a verb indicates when the action of the verb   1
takes place: at the present time, in the past, or in the future.

> I am studying PRESENT
> I studied   PAST
> I will study   FUTURE

As you can see in the above examples, just by putting the
verb in a different tense and without giving any additional information (such as "I am studying *now*," "I studied
yesterday," "I will study *tomorrow*"), you can indicate when
the action of the verb takes place.   10

Tenses may be classified according to the way they are
formed. A SIMPLE TENSE consists of only one verb form (I
studied), while a COMPOUND TENSE consists of one or more
auxiliaries plus the main verb (I *am studying*).

In this section we will only consider tenses of the
indicative mood (see *What is Meant by Mood?*, p. 71).

IN ENGLISH ───

Listed below are the main tenses of the indicative mood
whose equivalents you will encounter in German:
                                                                 20
> PRESENT
> > I study   PRESENT
> > I do study   PRESENT EMPHATIC
> > I am studying PRESENT PROGRESSIVE
> PAST
> > I studied   SIMPLE PAST
> > I did study   PAST EMPHATIC
> > I have studied PRESENT PERFECT
> > I was studying PAST PROGRESSIVE
> > I had studied PAST PERFECT
> FUTURE   30
> > I will study   FUTURE
> > I will have studied FUTURE PERFECT

As you can see, there are only two simple tenses (present
and simple past). All the other tenses are compound tenses.

IN GERMAN ───────────────────────────────

Listed below are the main tenses of the indicative mood that you will encounter in German.

PRESENT

ich studiere	*I study, I do study*	PRESENT
	I am studying	

PAST

ich studierte	{ *I studied,*	SIMPLE PAST/
	I was studying	IMPERFECT
ich habe studiert	*I have studied*	PRESENT PERFECT
ich hatte studiert	*I had studied*	PAST PERFECT

FUTURE

ich werde studieren	*I will study*	FUTURE
ich werde studiert haben	*I will have studied*	FUTURE PERFECT

As you can see, there are fewer present tense forms in German than in English. The compound tenses in German are formed with the auxiliary verbs **haben** *(to have)* or **sein** *(to be)* and **werden** *(to become)* + the main verb (see *What are Auxiliary Verbs?*, p. 76).

This handbook discusses the various tenses and their usage in separate chapters: *What is the Present Tense?*, p. 79; *What is the Past Tense?*, p. 81; *What is the Future Tense?*, p. 87; and *What are the Perfect Tenses?*, p. 83. Verb tenses can be grouped according to the mood in which they are used.

CAREFUL—Do not assume that tenses with the same name are used the same way in English and in German.

WHAT IS MEANT BY MOOD?

The word MOOD is a variation of the word *mode*, 1
meaning manner or way. The mood is expressed
    by a form of the verb that indicates
      the attitude of the speaker toward
        what he or she is saying.
As a beginning student of German, you need to know the
names of the moods so that you will understand what
your German textbook is referring to when it uses these
terms.

Verb forms are divided into moods, which, in turn, are
then subdivided into one or more tenses. You will learn 10
when to use the various moods as you learn verbs and
their tenses.

IN ENGLISH

Verbs can be in one of three moods:

INDICATIVE MOOD—The indicative mood is used to indicate
an action of the verb that really happens or is likely to
happen. This is the most common mood, and most of the
verb forms that you use in everyday conversation belong
to the indicative mood.

> Robert *studies* German. 20
> Mary *is* here.

The indicative mood occurs in the present tense (see
p. 79), the past tense (see p. 81), and the future tense (see
p. 87).

IMPERATIVE MOOD—The imperative mood is used to express
a command. The imperative mood does not have different tenses (see p. 73).

> Robert, *study* German now!
> Mary, *be* here on time! 30

SUBJUNCTIVE MOOD—The subjunctive mood is used to
express an attitude or feeling about the action of the verb.
The subjunctive mood has different tense forms (see
p. 147).

> I wish she *were* here.
> If only we *knew* where they are.
> The teacher recommended that they *do* the exercise.

IN GERMAN ─────────────────────────────

40

These same three moods exist and have their own special forms. As in English, the indicative is the most common mood; the subjunctive, however, is much more frequently used in German.

─ *REVIEW* ─

Imagine how a speaker might say each sentence and indicate the mood of the verbs in italics: indicative (I), imperative (IM), or subjunctive (S).

1. Columbus *discovered* America.   I   IM   S

2. We wish you *were* here.   I   IM   S

3. *Come* into the house, children!   I   IM   S

4. We *have* bats in the attic.   I   IM   S

5. *Look* at that!   I   IM   S

WHAT IS THE IMPERATIVE?

The **IMPERATIVE** is used to give someone an order.   1

> *Come* here!
> *Don't come* here!

IN ENGLISH ──────────────────────────────

There are two types of commands, depending on who is told to do, or not to do, something.

1. "You" **COMMAND**—When an order is given to one or more persons, the dictionary form of the verb is used.

   > *Answer* the phone.
   > *Clean* your room.   10
   > *Speak* softly.

2. "We" **COMMAND**—When an order is given to oneself as well as to others, the phrase "let's" (a contraction of *let us*) is used + the dictionary form of the verb.

   > *Let's leave.*
   > *Let's go* to the movies.

The absence of the pronoun in the sentence is a good indication that you are dealing with an imperative and not a present tense.   20

> *You answer* the phone.
> |
>   present
>
> *Answer* the phone.
> |
>   imperative

IN GERMAN──────────────────────────────

As in English, there are two types of imperatives, depending on who is being told to do or not to do something.

───────────── "You" **COMMAND** ─────────────   30

The *you*-command has three different forms, according to the three different personal pronouns for *you*: familiar, **du**, **ihr**, and formal, **Sie** (see *What is a Personal Pronoun?*, p. 19). In all forms except the **du**-form, the verb is the same as the present tense indicative. In written German an exclamation mark is used after an imperative.

1. DU-FORM—When an order is given to a person to whom you say **du**, the imperative is formed by using the stem of the verb; some verbs add the ending **-e**.

    Höre!
    Listen.

    Schreib mir bald!
    Write me soon.

2. IHR-FORM—When an order is given to two or more persons to whom you say **du** individually, the form of the verb is the same as the present tense indicative.

    Kommt mit!
    Come along.

    Esst nicht so schnell, Kinder!
    Don't eat so fast, children.

    Note that, as in English the subject pronoun is usually dropped.

3. SIE-FORM—When an order is given to one or more persons to whom you say **Sie** individually, the subject pronoun **Sie** is placed directly after the **Sie** form of the verb in the present tense.

    Sprechen Sie lauter!
    Speak more loudly.

    Kommen Sie mit!
    Come along.

─────────── "WE" COMMAND ───────────

When an order is given to oneself as well as to others, the subject pronoun **wir** is placed directly after the 1ˢᵗ person plural form of the verb in the present tense.

    Gehen wir jetzt!
    Let's go now.

    Sprechen wir Deutsch!
    Let's speak German.

Your German textbook will explain in detail the rules for forming the imperative.

— *REVIEW* —

Indicate the imperative form you would use when translating these sentences into German: **du, ihr, Sie**, or **wir**.

1. Hurry up, Chris.   DU   IHR   SIE   WIR

2. Let's go to the movies.   DU   IHR   SIE   WIR

3. Close the door, children.   DU   IHR   SIE   WIR

4. Excuse me a minute, Dr. Benn. DU   IHR   SIE   WIR

5. Please pick up your room, Ann. DU   IHR   SIE   WIR

CHAPTER

WHAT ARE AUXILIARY VERBS?

A verb is called an AUXILIARY VERB or HELPING VERB when
it helps another verb, called the MAIN VERB,
to form one of its tenses.

He *has been gone* two weeks. *has* AUXILIARY VERB
                                    been AUXILIARY VERB
                                      gone MAIN VERB

A verb tense composed of an auxiliary verb plus a main
verb is called a COMPOUND TENSE, as opposed to a SIMPLE
TENSE which is a tense composed of only the main verb.

Julia *had studied* for the exam.

auxiliary main
verb   verb
compound tense

Julia *studies* for the exam.

simple tense

IN ENGLISH

There are three auxiliary verbs, *to have, to be*, and *to do*,
as well as a series of auxiliary words, called MODALS, such
as *will, would, may, must, can, could,* that are used to
change the tense or meaning of the main verb.

- Auxiliary verbs are used primarily to indicate the tense
  of the main verb.

  Mary *is reading* a book.

  auxiliary *to be* + present participle of *to read*
  present progressive

  Mary *has written* a book.

  auxiliary *to have* + past participle of *to write*
  present perfect

- The auxiliary verb *to do* is used to help formulate questions and to make sentences negative.

  Does Mary *read* a book?
  Mary *does not read* a book.

- The auxiliary verb *to be* is used to indicate the verb is in
  the passive voice (see *What is Meant by Active and Passive
  Voice?*, p. 152).

The book *is read* by many people.

- The modal *will* is used to indicate the future tense

  Mary **will** *read* a book.
  |
  modal *will*

- Most modals are used to change the meaning of the main verb

  Mary **may** *read* a book.
  Mary **must** *read* a book.
  Mary **can** *read* a book.

IN GERMAN ────────────────────────────────

The three main auxiliary verbs are **haben** *(to have)*, **sein** *(to be)*, and **werden** *(to become)*. Like auxiliary verbs in English they are used to indicate tense (see *What are the Perfect Tenses?*, p. 83 and *What is the Future Tense?*, p. 87). The auxiliary **werden** is also used to indicate the passive voice (see *What is Meant by Active and Passive Voice?*, p. 152).

German modals are verbs which are used primarily to change the meaning of the main verb. Conjugated in all the tenses, German modals are followed by the infinitive of the main verb.

In the examples below, the action expressed by the main verb **lesen** *(to read)* is not actually occurring; its meaning is modified in a variety of ways depending on the modal auxiliary verb.

- **können** *(to be able, can)*
  Chris **kann** dieses Buch **lesen**.
  *Chris **can read** this book.*
  [Chris *has the ability to read* the book.]

- **dürfen** *(to be permitted to, may)*
  Chris **darf** dieses Buch **lesen**.
  *Chris **may read** this book.*
  [Chris *is allowed to read* the book.]

- **müssen** *(to be obligated to, must)*
  Chris **muß** dieses Buch **lesen**.
  *Chris **must read** this book.*
  [Chris *has to read* the book.]

- **sollen** *(to be supposed to, should)*
  Chris **soll** dieses Buch **lesen**.
  *Chris **should read** this book.*
  [Chris *ought to read* the book.]

CAREFUL—When you learn the modal verbs in German, especially **wollen** *(to want to)* and **mögen** *(to like to)*, pay attention to their definitions because they are not always equivalent in meaning to English modal verbs. Your textbook will explain the meanings of the German modal verbs and give you examples of how they are used.

— REVIEW —

I. Circle the auxiliary verbs and modals in the following English sentences.

- Cross out the English auxiliaries that will not be expressed as auxiliaries in a German sentence.
- On the line below indicate the verbs that will be expressed in a German sentence.

1. They are working on the problem.

———————————————

2. We can go now.

———————————————

3. You do have a point.

———————————————

4. She has waited a long time.

———————————————

5. He will arrive later.

———————————————

WHAT IS THE PRESENT TENSE?

The PRESENT TENSE indicates that the action is happening   1
at the present time. It can be at the moment the speaker
is speaking, a habitual action, or a general truth.

> I *see* you.
> He *smokes* when he *is* nervous.
> The sun *rises* every day.

IN ENGLISH

There are three verb forms that indicate the present tense.
Each form has a slightly different meaning:

> Maria *studies* in the library.   PRESENT   10
> Maria *is studying* in the library.   PRESENT PROGRESSIVE
> Maria *does study* in the library.   PRESENT EMPHATIC

Depending on the way a question is worded, you will
automatically choose one of the three above forms.

> Where does Mary study? She *studies* in the library.
> Where is Mary now? She *is studying* in the library.
> Does Mary study in the library? Yes, she *does* [*study* in the
> library].

IN GERMAN   20

Unlike English, there is only one verb form to indicate the
present tense. The German present tense is used to express
the meaning of the English present, present progressive,
and present emphatic tenses. The present tense in
German is a simple tense formed by adding a set of endings to the stem of the verb (see *What is a Verb
Conjugation?*, p. 41). Your textbook will give you the present tense endings.

> Maria *studies* in the library.   30
>   studiert
>
> Maria *is studying* in the library.
>   studiert
>
> Maria *does study* in the library.
>   studiert

— *REVIEW* —

Circle the words that correspond to the German present tense.

1. So John and Vera really do play tennis.

2. Yes, John plays often.

3. In fact, Vera is playing right now too.

4. Our friends are playing with them.

5. Do you play too?

WHAT IS THE PAST TENSE?

The PAST TENSE is used to express an action [1]
that occurred in the past.

I saw you yesterday.

IN ENGLISH

There are several verb forms that indicate the past tense

I worked	SIMPLE PAST
I was working	PAST PROGRESSIVE
I used to work	WITH HELPING VERB USED TO
I did work	PAST EMPHATIC
I have worked	PRESENT PERFECT [10]
I had worked	PAST PERFECT

The simple past is a simple tense; that is, it consists of one word (*worked* in the example above). The other past tenses are compound tenses; that is, they consist of more than one word, an auxiliary plus a main verb (*was working, did work*). The present and past perfect tenses are discussed in a separate section (see *What are the Perfect Tenses?*, p. 83).

IN GERMAN

There are two tenses most commonly used for expressing an [20] action in the past: the simple past and the present perfect.

SIMPLE PAST—The simple past, also called the IMPERFECT (Imperfekt), or the PRETERITE (Präteritum), consists of only one word.

Ich **arbeitete**	*I worked*
Ich **schwamm**	*I swam*

PRESENT PERFECT—The present perfect tense (**Perfekt**) is a compound tense, consisting of two parts: the auxiliary verbs **haben** *(to have)* or **sein** *(to be)* conjugated in the pre- [30] sent tense + the past participle of the main verb (see *What are Auxiliary Verbs?*, p. 76 and *What is a Participle?*, p. 89).

Ich **habe gearbeitet**	*I worked; I have worked*
Ich **bin geschwommen**	*I swam; I have swum*

The formation of both the simple past and the present perfect depends on whether the verb is categorized as a strong verb or a weak verb (see p. 67). Your German text-book will explain in detail the formation of these two tenses for both groups of verbs.

CAREFUL—It is important to remember that the simple past and the present perfect have equivalent meanings in German. Their difference is one of style and usage: gener-ally, the simple past is used in written German and the perfect in spoken German.

— REVIEW —

Underline the verb form(s) in the following sentences.
- Indicate whether the verb is in the simple past (SP) or the present perfect (PP).

1. Last summer I went to Germany
with my family.　　　　　　　　　　SP　PP

2. My mother has visited Germany many times.　SP　PP

3. Our trip was fun and interesting.　　SP　PP

4. We travelled around for two weeks.　SP　PP

5. I have shown my vacation
photos to my German class.　　　　SP　PP

WHAT ARE THE PERFECT TENSES?

The PERFECT TENSES are compound verbs made up of   1
the auxiliary verb *to have* + the past participle of
the main verb (see *What is a Participle?*, p. 89).

> I *have* not *seen* him.
> | |
> auxiliary   past participle
> verb   of *to see*

> They *had* already *gone*.
> | |
> auxiliary   past participle
> verb   of *to go*

IN ENGLISH ────────────────────   10

There are three perfect tenses formed with the auxiliary
verb *to have* + the past participle of the main verb. The
name of each perfect tense is based on the tense used for
the auxiliary verb *to have*.

1. **PRESENT PERFECT**—*to have* in the present tense + the past
participle of the main verb (see *What is the Present Tense?*,
p. 79).

> I *have eaten*.
> | |
> present   past participle
>   of *to eat*   20

> The boys *have washed* the car.
> | |
>   present   past participle
>   of *to wash*

2. **PAST PERFECT (PLUPERFECT)**—*to have* in the simple past +
the past participle of the main verb (see *What is the Past
Tense?*, p. 81). The past perfect is used to express an
action completed in the past before some other past
action or event.   30

> I *had eaten* before six.
> | |
> simple   past participle
> past   of *to eat*

> The boys *had washed* the car before the storm.
> | |
>   simple   past participle
>   past   of *to wash*

3. **FUTURE PERFECT**—*to have* in the future tense + past participle of the main verb (see *What is the Future Tense?*, p. 87). The future perfect expresses an action which will be completed in the future before some other action or event occurs in the future.

> I *will have eaten.*
> future   past participle
> of *to eat*

> The boys *will have washed* the car by Thursday.
> future   past participle
> of *to wash*

IN GERMAN

As in English, there are three perfect tenses in the indicative mood (see *What is Meant by Mood?*, p. 71). The perfect tenses use a form of the auxiliary verb **haben** *(to have)* or **sein** *(to be)* + the past participle of the main verb. You must memorize which verbs require **sein** and which require **haben** as the auxiliary. As in English, the name of the tense reflects the tense of the auxiliary verb.

We are listing the various perfect tenses here so that you can see the pattern they follow. The perfect tenses are not always used in the same way in German as in English. Consult your German textbook in order to learn how to use them properly.

1. **PERFECT** (PERFEKT)—**haben** *(to have)* or **sein** *(to be)* in the present tense + past participle of the main verb.

> Wir **sind** ins Kino **gegangen.**
> We *have gone* to the movies.
> present perfect
> We *went* to the movies.
> simple past

> Wir **haben** den Film **gesehen.**
> We *have seen* the film.
> present perfect
> We *saw* the film.
> simple past

Note that although the perfect in German has a similar structure to the English present perfect, using the simple past in English results in a better translation.

2. PAST PERFECT OR PLUPERFECT (PLUSQUAMPERFEKT)—**haben** *(to have)* or **sein** *(to be)* in the simple past tense + past participle of the main verb.

> Wir **waren** schon ins Kino **gegangen**.
>
> simple past of **sein** *(to be)* past participle of **gehen** *(to go)*
>
> *We **had** already **gone** to the movies.*
>
> Wir **hatten** den Film schon **gesehen**.
>
> simple past of **haben** *(to have)* past participle of **sehen** *(to see)*
>
> *We **had** already **seen** the film.*

Generally, the German past perfect is used the same way as the past perfect in English: to express an action or condition that ended before some other past action or condition which may or may not be stated. Notice how we can express the sequence of events by using different tenses.

Verb tense:	Pluperfect -2	Perfect or Simple past -1	Present 0
Time action takes place:	before -1	before 0	now

> *They **had** already **left** when I **arrived**.*
> Sie **waren** schon **abgefahren**, als ich **ankam**.
>
> pluperfect -2   simple past -1

3. FUTURE PERFECT TENSE—**haben** *(to have)* or **sein** *(to be)* in the future tense + past participle of the main verb.

> Wir **werden** den Film **gesehen haben**.
>
> future tense of **haben** *(to have)*
>
> *We **will have seen** the film.*

Generally, the German future perfect is used the same way as the future perfect in English: to express an action which will be completed in the future before some other future action or event, which may or may not be stated. Notice how we can express the sequence of events by using different tenses.

Verb tense:	Present 0	Future perfect 1	Future 2
Time action takes place:	now	after 0 before 2	after 0 and after 1

*They **will have left** before I arrive.*
Sie **werden abgefahren sein,** bevor ich ankomme.

future perfect (1)   event in the future (2)

Both action (1) and event (2) will occur at some future time, but action (1) will be completed before event (2) takes place. Therefore, action (1) is in the future perfect tense.

130   You will have to learn to recognize these tenses because they indicate the sequence in which events take place.

— REVIEW —

Circle the tense of the verb in italics: perfect (P), pluperfect (PP), or future perfect (FP).

1. We *had* already *gone*
   when Katie arrived.   P   PP   FP

2. Barbara *hasn't left* yet.   P   PP   FP

3. I *will have graduated*
   by next summer.   P   PP   FP

4. *Have* you *seen* my new car?   P   PP   FP

WHAT IS THE FUTURE TENSE?

The **FUTURE TENSE** indicates that an action will take place some time in the future.   1

> I *will return* the book as soon as I've read it.
>   └─┬─┘
>   future

IN ENGLISH

The future tense is formed with the auxiliary *will* or *shall* + the dictionary form of the main verb. In conversation *shall* and *will* are often shortened to *'ll*.

> Paul and Mary *will do* their homework tomorrow.   10
> *I'll leave* tonight.

An action that will take place in the future can also be expressed in the present tense with an adverb of future time or an expression of future time.

> Maria *is meeting* Paul *tomorrow.*
>   └──┬──┘   │
> present progressive   adverb
>
> Paul *goes* to Berlin *next week.*
>   │   └──┬──┘
> present   expression of future time   20

IN GERMAN

The future tense is formed with the auxiliary verb **werden** *(to become)* + the infinitive of the main verb. The verb **werden** is conjugated to agree with the subject and the infinitive remains unchanged. The infinitive is placed at the end of the sentence.

> Maria und Paul **werden** ihre Hausaufgabe **schreiben.**
>   │   │
>   3rd per. pl.   infinitive
> *Maria and Paul **will write** their homework.*   30
>
> Ich **werde** heute abend **ausgehen.**
>   │   │
> 1st per. sing.   infinitive
> *I **shall go out** tonight.*

As in English, an action that will take place in the future can also be expressed in the present tense with an adverb or an expression of future time.

Mary und Paul **schreiben morgen** ihre Prüfung.

present + adverb of future time

Mary and Paul are writing their test tomorrow.

Ich **gehe gleich.**

present + adverb of future time

I am going soon.

────────── **FUTURE OF PROBABILITY** ──────────

In addition to expressing an action that will take place in the future, the future tense in German can be used to express a probable fact, what the speaker feels is probably true. This is called the FUTURE OF PROBABILITY.

IN ENGLISH

The idea of probability is expressed in the present tense accompanied with words such as *must, probably, wonder.*

> My keys *must* be around here.
> My keys are *probably* around here.
> I *wonder* if my keys are around here.

IN GERMAN

Unlike English which uses the present tense + an adverb of probability, in German the future of probability is usually expressed with the future tense + an adverb such as **wohl** *(probably)*, **sicher** *(certainly)*, **wahrscheinlich** *(probably)*, and **vielleicht** *(perhaps)*.

> Sie **werden** dieses Buch **sicher kennen.**
>
> adverb (sicher) + future tense of **kennen** *(to know)*
>
> *You surely know this book.*
>
> adverb *(surely)* + present tense of *to know*

── *R E V I E W* ──

In the sentences below underline the verbs in future tense.
- Circle the verbs in the present tense which are used with an adverb of future time.

1. Next week we are going on vacation.

2. Erica will go downtown.

3. I shall return.

4. Tomorrow I am flying to Europe.

5. He'll be here in a minute.

WHAT IS A PARTICIPLE?

A **PARTICIPLE** is a form of a verb that can be used
in one of two ways: with an auxiliary verb to indicate
certain tenses, or as an adjective to describe something.

He *has closed* the door.

auxiliary + participle → past tense

He heard me through the *closed* door.

participle describing *door* → adjective

There are two types of participles: the present participle
and the past participle.

─────────────── **PRESENT PARTICIPLE** ───────────────

IN ENGLISH

The present participle is easy to recognize because it is the
-ing form of the verb: *working, studying, dancing, playing.*

The present participle has three primary uses:

1. as the main verb in compound tenses with the auxiliary
verb *to be* (see *What are Auxiliary Verbs?*, p. 76)

She *is writing* with her new pen.

present progressive of *to write*

They *were sleeping.*

past progressive of *to sleep*

2. as an adjective (see *What is a Descriptive Adjective?*,
p. 112)

The pen is a *writing* instrument.

describes the noun *instrument*

He woke the *sleeping* child.

describes the noun *child*

3. in a phrase (see p. 47)

Turning the corner, Tony ran into a tree.

phrase describing *Tony.*

IN GERMAN

The present participle is always formed by adding -**d** to the infinitive (see *What is an Infinitive?*, p. 26).

INFINITIVE	PRESENT PARTICIPLE
singen	singend
spielen	spielend
sprechen	sprechend

The present participle occurs less frequently in German than in English and it is not used in the same way. However, it is often used as an adjective that can take adjective endings.

> die **singenden** Kinder
> *the **singing** children*

> ein **spielendes** Mädchen
> *a **playing** girl*

CAREFUL—Never assume that an English word ending with -*ing* is translated by its German counterpart ending in -**d**. Keep in mind that English tenses formed with an auxiliary + present participle (she *is singing*, they *were dancing*) do not exist in German. These tenses are expressed by a one word German verb whose tense corresponds to the tense of the auxiliary.

> She **is singing.**
> |
> present
> Sie **singt.**
> |
> present

> They **were dancing.**
> |
> simple past
> Sie **tanzten.**
> |
> simple past

─────── **PRESENT PARTICIPLE VERSUS GERUND** ───────

An English verb ending in -*ing* is not always a present participle; it can be a verbal noun. A **VERBAL NOUN**, also called a **GERUND**, is the form of a verb which functions as a noun in a sentence: it can be a subject, a direct object, an indirect object, or an object of a preposition.

It is important that you learn to distinguish an English participle from a gerund since German gerunds differ in form from present participles.

IN ENGLISH   80

GERUND—A word ending in -*ing* is a gerund if you can use only one word to replace it in a question. The gerund will answer this one-word question.

> *Reading* can be fun.
>> *What* can be fun? Reading.
>> *Reading,* a noun derived from the verb *to read,* is the subject of the sentence.

> We have often thought about *moving* away.
>> We often thought about *what*? Moving.
>> *Moving,* a noun derived from the verb *to move,*   90
>> is the object of the preposition *about.*

PRESENT PARTICIPLE—A word ending in -*ing* is a present participle if you must use more than one word or the verb *to do* to replace it in a question. The present participle will answer this question.

> We are *singing.*
>> What *are we doing*? Singing.

> *Singing* is fun.
>> What *is fun?* Singing.   100
>> *Singing,* a noun derived from the verb *to sing,*
>> is a gerund.

IN GERMAN

Gerunds are usually expressed by a neuter noun made from the infinitive of the verb.

> lesen   *to read*   →   **das** Lesen   *reading*
> singen *to sing*   →   **das** Singen *singing*

As you can see in the examples below, knowing how to distinguish a gerund from a present participle will enable you to select the correct form for German.   110

> *We **are talking** a lot.*
>> *What are we doing*? Talking.
>> *Talking* is a present participle used in the present tense.
> Wir **reden** viel.
>> |
>> verb

> *Talking is silver, **being silent** is gold.* ["Silence is golden."]
>> *What* is silver? Talking.
>> *What* is gold? Being silent.
>> *Talking* and *being silent* are gerunds.   120
> **Reden** ist Silber, **Schweigen** ist Gold.
>> | | | |
>> gerund verb   gerund   verb

In German, it is easy to identify a gerund since all German nouns are capitalized.

──────────────── **PAST PARTICIPLE** ────────────────
IN ENGLISH

The past participle is formed in several ways. It is the form of the verb that follows the various forms of the auxiliary *to have*: I *have* **spoken**, he *has* **written**, we *have* **walked**.

The past participle has three primary uses:

1. as the main verb in perfect tenses with the auxiliary verb *to have* (see *What are the Perfect Tenses?*, p. 83)

> I *have written* all that I have to say.
> └────┬────┘
> present perfect of *to write*

> He *had*n't *spoken* to me all day.
> └────┬────┘
> past perfect of *to speak*

2. as the main verb in passive voice with the auxiliary verb *to be* (see *What is Meant by Active and Passive Voice?*, p. 152)

> That book *was written* last year.
> └────┬────┘
> past passive

> That language *is* no longer *spoken*.
> └────┬────┘
> present passive

3. as an adjective (see *What is a Descriptive Adjective?*, p. 112)

> Is the *written* word more important than the *spoken* word?
>   │   │
> describes the noun *word*   describes the noun *word*

IN GERMAN

The past participle is formed differently depending on whether the verb is weak or strong (see p. 67). While all weak verbs form their past participle according to the same rule, strong verbs have irregular past participles which must be memorized.

WEAK VERBS—The past participles of weak verbs are formed by adding a prefix and a suffix (see *What are Prefixes and Suffixes?*, p. 28). The prefix **ge-** is added to the front of the stem and the suffix **-t** is added to the end of the stem.

INFINITIVE	STEM	PAST PARTICIPLE	
machen	mach-	gemacht	*made*
glauben	glaub-	geglaubt	*believed*

Some verb stems require slight adjustments. There are special rules for forming the past participle of verbs that already begin with prefixes and for verbs that end with the suffix **-ieren.** Your German textbook will explain how to handle these verbs.

STRONG VERBS—The past participles of strong verbs often change the stem vowel, and occasionally some of the consonants. The prefix **ge-** is added to the front of the stem, unless the verb already begins with an inseparable prefix (see p. 29), and the ending is **-en** (or **-n**).

INFINITIVE	PAST PARTICIPLE	
schlafen	geschlafen	*slept*
gehen	gegangen	*gone*
finden	gefunden	*found*
liegen	gelegen	*lain*

As with weak verbs, there are special rules for forming the past participle of strong verbs that already begin with a prefix. Since there is no way to predict the past participle of a strong verb, you will have to memorize it when you learn the verb.

Remember that the past participle of strong verbs always ends in **-en** (or **-n**), while the past participle of weak verbs always ends in **-t.**

As in English, the past participle can be used in the perfect tenses, in the passive, and as an adjective.

1. as the main verb in the perfect tenses: **haben** *(to have)* or **sein** *(to be)* + the past participle

> Ich **habe** das Buch **gelesen.**
> *I **have read** the book.*
> *I **read** the book.*

> Ich **bin** nach Hause **gekommen.**
> *I **have come** home.*
> *I **came** home.*

2. as the main verb in the passive voice: **werden** *(to become)* + the past participle (see *What is Meant by Active and Passive Voice?*, p. 152)

> Das Buch **wird** von mir **gelesen.**
> *The book **is read** by me.*

3. as an adjective with adjective endings

> Ich lese den **getippten** Brief.
> *I read the **typed** letter.*

— *REVIEW* —

Circle the tense of the verb forms in italics: present participle (P) or past participle (PP).

1. At 10:00 p.m. John was *watching* TV.

    P   PP

2. We had already *gone* when Tom called.

    P   PP

3. An antique dealer near our house fixes *broken* china.

    P   PP

4. Mary is *studying* in the library right now.

    P   PP

WHAT IS AN INTERROGATIVE PRONOUN?

An **INTERROGATIVE PRONOUN** is a word that replaces a noun   1
and introduces a question. The word *interrogative*
comes from *interrogate,* to question.

> *Who* is coming for dinner?
> |
> question referring to a person
>
> *What* did you eat for dinner?
> |
> question referring to a thing

In both English and German, a different interrogative pronoun is used depending on whether it refers to a "person"
(human beings and live animals) or a "thing" (objects and   10
ideas). Also, the form of the interrogative pronoun often
changes according to its function in the sentence: subject,
direct object, indirect object, and object of a preposition.
We shall look at each type separately.

— INTERROGATIVE PRONOUNS REFERRING TO A PERSON —
"WHO, WHOM, WHOSE"

IN ENGLISH

Who is used for the subject of the sentence.
                                                              20
> *Who* lives here?
> |
> subject
>
> *Who* are they?
> |
> subject

Whom is used for the direct object, indirect object, and
object of a preposition.

> *Whom* do you know here?
> |
> direct object
>   30
> *To whom* did you speak?
> |
> indirect object
>
> *From whom* did you get the book?
> |
> object of preposition *from*

Whose is the possessive form and is used to ask about possession or ownership.

There's a pencil on the floor? *Whose* is it?
                               |
                          possessive

They are nice cars. *Whose* are they?
                      |
                 possessive

In spoken English we often use the interrogative pronoun *who* instead of *whom*. This makes it difficult to identify its function: is it the subject or an object? It is only by asking the proper questions that you will find the function.

> *Who* do you know here?
> VERB: know
> FIND SUBJECT: *Who* knows? You.
>   *You* is the subject.
> FUNCTION OF *WHO*: an object
> *Whom* do you know here?

IN GERMAN

There are four forms of interrogative pronouns depending on the case required. Number and gender do not affect interrogative pronouns in German.

To select the proper form of the interrogative pronoun, you will have to determine its function in the German sentence by asking the following five questions:

1. Is it the subject of the question?
2. Is it the object of the German verb? Does that verb take the accusative or dative?
3. Is it the indirect object of the verb?
4. Is it the object of a preposition? If so, does that German preposition take the accusative or dative?
5. Is it the possessive pronoun *whose?*

───── "WHO?" (SUBJECT) → "WER?" (NOMINATIVE) ─────

Be sure to establish that *who* functions as the subject of the question and not the object. (To help you establish function, see "dangling prepositions," p. 98.)

Wer—The nominative form can refer to both singular and plural subjects.

> *Who is in the room? The teacher is in the room.*
> **Wer** ist in dem Zimmer? Die Lehrerin ist in dem Zimmer.

> *Who is coming this evening? Hans and Inge are coming.*
> **Wer** kommt heute abend? Hans und Inge kommen.

—— "WHOM?" (OBJECT) → "WEN?" (ACCUSATIVE) ——
OR "WEM?" (DATIVE)

Once you have established that the interrogative pronoun is an object, you will need to determine whether the accusative or dative case is required in German.

Wen—The accusative form is used after verbs that require an accusative direct object and after prepositions that require an accusative object.

> *Whom do you see?*
> **Wen** sehen Sie?
>
> |
> direct object

> *For whom is the letter?*
> **Für wen** ist der Brief?
>
> |
> preposition **für** *(for)* requires accusative object

Wem—The dative form is used for indirect objects, after prepositions that require a dative object, and after the few verbs that require a dative direct object.

> *To whom did you tell the story?*
> **Wem** hast du die Geschichte erzählt?
>
> |
> indirect object

> *With whom are you coming?*
> **Mit wem** kommst du?
>
> |
> preposition **mit** *(with)* requires dative object

> *Whom are they helping?*
> **Wem** helfen sie?
>
> |
> verb **helfen** *(to help)* requires dative direct object

Note that when **wem** functions as an object it means "to whom" or "for whom" and the German prepositions "to" or "for" do not need to be expressed.

> *Whom are you doing a favor for?*
> **Wem** tust du einen Gefallen?
>
> |
> indirect object

However, when **wem** functions as the object of any other preposition besides "to" and "for," it is not an indirect object and the German preposition must be expressed. (To learn how to identify interrogative pronouns that are objects of a preposition, see "dangling prepositions," p. 98.)

With whom are we going?
Mit wem gehen wir?

—— **"WHOSE?" (POSSESSIVE)** → **"WESSEN?" (GENITIVE)** ———
Wessen—There is only one form in German for the possessive interrogative pronoun *whose*.

Wessen Bleistift ist das?
Whose pencil is that?

Wessen Haus habt ihr gekauft?
Whose house did you buy?

————————— **DANGLING PREPOSITIONS** —————————
(see *What is a Preposition?*, p. 126)

IN ENGLISH

In English it is difficult to identify the function of interrogative pronouns that are objects of a preposition because the pronouns are often separated from the preposition of which they are the object: the interrogative pronoun is placed at the beginning of the question and the preposition at the end. Consequently, in conversation the interrogative subject pronoun *who* is often used instead of the interrogative object pronoun *whom*.

Who did you give the book *to?*
   | |
interrogative   dangling preposition
pronoun

When a preposition is separated from its object, it is called a **DANGLING PREPOSITION**.

To enable you to establish the function of an interrogative pronoun, you will have to change the structure of the question so that the preposition is placed before the interrogative pronoun. In formal English there is a tendency to avoid dangling prepositions.

| **SPOKEN ENGLISH** | → | **FORMAL ENGLISH** |

Who did you speak *to?*   *To whom* did you speak?
 | |
instead of *whom* preposition

Who did you get the book *from?* *From whom* did you get the book?
 | |
instead of *whom*   preposition

IN GERMAN

German places prepositions in the same position as formal English; that is, at the beginning of a question. By restructuring English questions with dangling prepositions you will not only be able to identify the function of interrogative pronouns, but also establish the word order for the German sentence.

Here are a few examples of questions with interrogative pronouns which have been restructured to avoid the dangling preposition.

Who is she writing to? → *To whom is she writing?*

subject form of   preposition   object form of interr. pronoun
interr. pronoun

Wem schreibt sie?

dative

Who are you leaving with? → *With whom are you leaving?*

subject form of   preposition   object form of interr. pronoun
interr. pronoun

Mit wem gehst du?

dative

Who are you waiting for? → *For whom are you waiting?*

subject form of   preposition   object form of interr. pronoun
interr. pronoun

Auf wen wartest du?

accusative

— INTERROGATIVE PRONOUN REFERRING TO A THING—
"WHAT"

IN ENGLISH

What refers only to things or ideas. The same form is used for subject, direct object, indirect object, and the object of a preposition.

What happened?

subject

What do you want?

direct object

What is the movie about?

object of preposition *about*

IN GERMAN

As in English there is only one form of interrogative pronoun to refer to things, **was** *(what)*.

Was ist in diesem Paket?
What is in this package?

Was machst du?
What are you doing?

210

———————————— **SUMMARY** ————————————

Here is a chart you can use as reference.

INTERROGATIVE PRONOUN		
REFERRING TO PERSONS		
NOMINATIVE	wer	*who*
ACCUSATIVE	wen	*whom*
DATIVE	wem	*whom*
GENITIVE	wessen	*whose*
REFERRING TO THINGS	was	*what*

— *REVIEW* —

I. Underline the interrogative pronouns in the following sentences, restructuring where appropriate.
- Indicate the type and function of the antecedent: subject (S), direct object (DO), indirect object (ID), or object of a preposition (OP).
- Write the appropriate German interrogative pronoun using the information given.

1. Who read the book?

TYPE OF ANTECEDENT:	Person	Thing		
FUNCTION:	S	DO	IO	OP

_____ hat das Buch gelesen?

2. What did she say?

TYPE OF ANTECEDENT:	Person	Thing		
FUNCTION:	S	DO	IO	OP

_____ hat sie gesagt?

3. Whose car is that?

TYPE OF ANTECEDENT:	Person	Thing		
FUNCTION:	S	DO	IO	OP

_____ Auto ist das?

4. Who are we waiting for?

TYPE OF ANTECEDENT:	Person	Thing		
FUNCTION:	S	DO	IO	OP

(*to wait for* = **warten auf** + accusative)

Auf _____ warten wir?

WHAT IS A POSSESSIVE PRONOUN?

A **POSSESSIVE PRONOUN** is a word that replaces a noun
and indicates the possessor of that noun. The word
possessive comes from *possess,* to own.

1

> Whose house is that? It's *mine.*
> replaces the noun *house,* the object possessed,
> and shows who possesses it, *me*

IN ENGLISH

Here is a list of the possessive pronouns:

SINGULAR POSSESSOR		
1ST PERSON		mine
2ND PERSON		yours
3RD PERSON	MASCULINE	his
	FEMININE	hers
	NEUTER	its
PLURAL POSSESSOR		
1ST PERSON		ours
2ND PERSON		yours
3RD PERSON		theirs

10

The pronouns refer to the possessor, not the possessed.

20

> My car is red; what color is John's? *His* is blue.
> 3rd pers. masc. sing.

> John's car is blue. What color is yours? *Mine* is white.
> 1st pers. sing.

> Although the object possessed is the same *(car),* different
> possessive pronouns *(his* and *mine)* are used because the
> possessors are different *(John* and *me).*

> Is that John's house? Yes, it is *his.*
> Are those John's keys? Yes, they are *his.*

30

> Although the objects possessed are different *(house* and
> *keys),* the same possessive pronoun *(his)* is used because
> the possessor is the same *(John).*

IN GERMAN

Like English, a German possessive pronoun refers to the
possessor. Unlike English, and like all German pronouns,

40　　it also agrees in gender and number with the antecedent, that is, with the person or object possessed. In addition, the appropriate case endings are added to the possessive pronoun to reflect its function in the sentence.

Let us look at the German possessive pronouns to which the case endings are added.

SINGULAR POSSESSOR

1ST PERSON		mein-	*mine*
2ND PERSON	INFORMAL	dein-	*yours*
	FORMAL	Ihr-	*yours*
3RD PERSON	MASCULINE	sein-	*his*
	FEMININE	ihr-	*hers*
	NEUTER	sein-	*its*

PLURAL POSSESSOR

1ST PERSON		unser-	*ours*
2ND PERSON	INFORMAL	euer-	*yours*
	FORMAL	Ihr-	*yours*
3RD PERSON		ihr-	*theirs*

The forms of the possessive pronouns are essentially the same as those of the possessive adjectives (see *What is a Possessive Adjective?*, p. 104). Possessive adjectives are more commonly used in German than the possessive pronoun. Your textbook will explain how to recognize possessive pronouns.

— REVIEW —

Circle the possessive pronouns in the following sentences.

1. I have my book; do you have yours?

2. Did your parents come? Ours stayed home.

3. Whose report was the best? Hers was.

4. Did somebody forget this jacket? Yes, it's his.

5. Let me see those keys: I bet they're mine.

31. WHAT IS AN ADJECTIVE?

An ADJECTIVE is a word that describes a noun or a pronoun.
There are different types of adjectives;
they are classified according to the way
they describe a noun or pronoun.

DESCRIPTIVE ADJECTIVE—A descriptive adjective indicates a quality; it tells what kind of noun it is (see p. 112).
> She read an *interesting* book.
> He has *brown* eyes.

POSSESSIVE ADJECTIVE— A possessive adjective shows possession; it tells whose noun it is (see p. 104).
> *His* book is lost.
> *Our* parents are away.

INTERROGATIVE ADJECTIVE—An interrogative adjective asks a question about a noun (see p. 109).
> *What* book is lost?
> *Which* book did you read?

DEMONSTRATIVE ADJECTIVE—A demonstrative adjective points out a noun (see p. 107).
> *This* teacher is excellent.
> *That* question is very appropriate.

IN ENGLISH ———————————————
English adjectives usually do not change their form, regardless of the noun or pronouns described.

IN GERMAN ———————————————
While English adjectives do not change their form, German adjectives change in order to agree with the case, gender, and number of the noun they modify. The various types of adjectives are discussed in separate sections.

CHAPTER

WHAT IS A POSSESSIVE ADJECTIVE?

A **POSSESSIVE ADJECTIVE** is a word that describes a noun by showing who possesses that noun.

Whose house is that? It's *my* house.

> *My* shows who possesses the noun *house*. The possessor is "me." The object possessed is *house*.

IN ENGLISH ————————————————————————

Like subject pronouns, possessive adjectives are identified according to the person they represent (see p. 19).

SINGULAR POSSESSOR

1ST PERSON		my
2ND PERSON		your
3RD PERSON	MASCULINE	his
	FEMININE	her
	NEUTER	its

PLURAL POSSESSOR

1ST PERSON	our
2ND PERSON	your
3RD PERSON	their

A possessive adjective changes to identify the possessor, regardless of the objects possessed.

Is that John's house? Yes, it is *his* house.
Is that Mary's house? Yes, it is *her* house.

> Although the object possessed is the same *(house)*, different possessive adjectives *(his* and *her)* are used because the possessors are different *(John* and *Mary)*.

Is that John's house? Yes, it is *his* house.
Are those John's keys? Yes, they are *his* keys.

> Although the objects possessed are different *(house* and *keys)*, the same possessive adjective *(his)* is used because the possessor is the same *(John)*.

IN GERMAN ————————————————————————

Like English, a German possessive adjective changes to identify the possessor, but unlike English it also agrees in case, gender and number with the noun possessed.

To choose the correct form of the possessive adjective follow these steps:

1. Find the possessor.

SINGULAR POSSESSOR

1ST PERSON		mein-	*my*
2ND PERSON	FAMILIAR	dein-	*your*
	MASCULINE	sein-	*his*
3RD PERSON	FEMININE	ihr-	*her*
	NEUTER	sein-	*its*

PLURAL POSSESSOR

1ST PERSON		unser-	*our*
2ND PERSON	FAMILIAR	euer-	*your*
	FORMAL	Ihr-	*your*
3RD PERSON		ihr-	*their*

2. Identify and analyze the noun possessed:

CASE—Is it nominative, accusative, dative or genitive?
GENDER— Is it masculine, feminine or neuter?
NUMBER— Is it singular or plural?

3. Add the ending for the possessive adjective that corresponds to the case, gender, and number of the noun possessed. These endings are the same as those for the indefinite articles, **ein**, **eine**, and **ein**, as shown in your textbook.

Let us apply the above steps to examples:

*He always forgets **his** books.*
1. POSSESSOR: *his* → sein-
2. NOUN POSSESSED: *books*
   CASE: **vergessen** *(to forget)* takes a direct object → accusative
   GENDER: **das Buch** *(book)* is neuter
   NUMBER: *books* is plural
3. ENDING: accusative neuter, plural → **-e**
Er vergißt immer **seine** Bücher.

*She gives **her** brother the telephone number.*
1. POSSESSOR: *her* → ihr-
2. NOUN POSSESSED: *brother*
   CASE: indirect object of **geben** *(to give)* → dative
   (She gives her number *to whom?* Her brother.)
   GENDER: **der Bruder** *(brother)* is masculine
   NUMBER: *brother* is singular
3. ENDING: dative masculine singular → **-em**
Sie gibt **ihrem** Bruder die Telefonnummer.

CAREFUL – Remember that **ihr-** with an ending and followed by a noun is a possessive adjective that can mean *her*, *their* or *your* (formal) depending on possessor. If **ihr**

has no ending and is not in front of a noun, it is a pronoun and it can mean either *you* (familiar plural) or *her* (dative).

— REVIEW —

I. Underline the possessive adjective in the following sentences.
- Circle the noun possessed.

1. The students took their exams home.

2. Susan put on her coat and her scarf.

3. Tom put his comb in his pocket.

WHAT IS A DEMONSTRATIVE ADJECTIVE?

An **DEMONSTRATIVE ADJECTIVE** is a word used [1]
to point out a noun.

This book is interesting.
|
points out the noun *book*

IN ENGLISH

The demonstrative adjectives are *this* and *that* in the singular and *these* and *those* in the plural. They are rare examples of English adjectives agreeing in number with the noun they modify: *this* changes to *these* and *that* [10] changes to *those* when they modify a plural noun.

SINGULAR	PLURAL
this cat	*these* cats
that man	*those* men

This and *these* refer to persons or objects near the speaker, and *that* and *those* refer to persons or objects away from the speaker.

IN GERMAN

The stems of the demonstrative adjectives are **dies-** *(this)*, **jed-** *(each, every)* and **all-** *(these)*. Like all adjectives in [20] German, a demonstrative adjective changes form to agree in case, gender, and number with the noun it modifies. The endings added to the stem are the same as for the definite article (see *What are Articles?*, p. 13).

In order to choose the correct form of the demonstrative adjective, begin by analyzing the noun modified.

1. CASE: Is it nominative, accusative, or genitive?
2. GENDER: Is it masculine, feminine, or neuter?
3. NUMBER: Is it singular or plural? [30]
4. SELECTION: Refer to your textbook for the endings.

Let us apply the above steps to examples:

This *room is large.*
   CASE: subject of **sein** *(to be)* → nominative
   GENDER: **das Zimmer** *(room)* is neuter
   NUMBER: **das Zimmer** *(room)* is singular
   SELECTION: nominative neuter singular ending → -es
Dieses Zimmer ist gross.

40

*Show **every** person the house.*
> CASE: indirect object of **zeigen** *(to show)* → dative
> GENDER: **die Person** *(person)* is feminine
> NUMBER: **die Person** *(person)* is singular
> SELECTION: dative feminine singular ending → **-er**

Zeig **jeder** Person das Haus.

*I want to see **all** rooms in the house.*
> CASE: direct object of **sehen** *(to see)* → accusative
> GENDER: **das Zimmer** *(room)* is neuter
> NUMBER: **Zimmer** *(rooms)* is plural
> SELECTION: accusative neuter plural ending → **-e**

Ich will **alle** Zimmer im Haus sehen.

— REVIEW —

Circle the demonstative adjective in the sentences below.

- Draw an arrow from the demonstrative adjective to the noun it modifies.

1. Did you see every room?

2. I prefer this house.

3. All houses are expensive.

4. These windows are nice.

5. Thoses closets are large.

WHAT IS AN INTERROGATIVE ADJECTIVE?

An **INTERROGATIVE ADJECTIVE** is a word that asks for information about a noun.   1

> *Which* book do you want?
> |
> asks information about the noun *book*

IN ENGLISH

The words **which** and **what** are called interrogative adjectives when they come in front of a noun and are used to ask a question about that noun.

> *Which* instructor is teaching the course?   10
> *What* courses are you taking?

IN GERMAN

There is only one interrogative adjective, **welch-**. Like all adjectives in German, the ending changes to agree in case, gender, and number with the noun it modifies.

To choose the correct form of **welch-**:

1. Identify and analyze the noun modified.
   - What is its case? Is it nominative, accusative, dative   20
     or genitive?
   - What is its gender? Is it masculine, feminine or
     neuter?
   - What is its number? Is it singular or plural?

2. Provide the ending for **welch-** that corresponds to the
   case, gender, and number of the noun modified. These
   endings are the same as those for the definite articles
   (**der, die, das**), except in the neuter singular nominative and accusative where the ending -es replaces -as.
                                                                30
Let us apply the above steps to examples:

> *Which lamp is cheaper?*
>   1. NOUN MODIFIED: lamp
>   CASE: subject of **sein** *(to be)* → nominative
>   GENDER: **die Lampe** *(lamp)* is feminine
>   NUMBER: *lamp* is singular
>   2. ENDING: nominative feminine singular → -e
> **Welche** Lampe ist billiger?

Which (what) dress do you want to wear?
1. NOUN MODIFIED: dress
   CASE: direct object of **tragen** *(to wear)* → accusative
   GENDER: **das Kleid** *(dress)* is neuter
   NUMBER: *dress* is singular
2. ENDING: accusative neuter singular → **-es**

Welches Kleid willst du tragen?

Which man do we give our tickets to?
1. NOUN MODIFIED: man
   CASE: indirect object of **geben** *(to give)* → dative
   GENDER: **der Mann** *(man)* is masculine
   NUMBER: *man* is singular
2. ENDING: dative masculine singular → **-em**

Welchem Mann geben wir unsere Karten?

──────── **INTERROGATIVE ADJECTIVE AS THE OBJECT OF A PREPOSITION** ────────

If the interrogative adjective is the object of a preposition, you must begin the question with the preposition followed by the interrogative adjective in the case required by that preposition. Remember to restructure dangling prepositions when expressing an English sentence in German. This will help you identify the object of the preposition and your sentence will correspond to the German sentence structure (see p. 98).

Which street does he live on? → *On which street does he live?*
1. NOUN MODIFIED: street
   CASE: object of preposition **in** *(in, on)* → dative
   GENDER: **die Straße** *(street)* is feminine
   NUMBER: *street* is singular
2. ENDING: dative feminine singular → **-er**

In welcher Straße wohnt er?

What film are you talking about? → *About what film are you talking?*
1. NOUN MODIFIED: film
   CASE: object of preposition **von** *(about)* → dative
   GENDER: **der Film** *(film)* is masculine
   NUMBER: *film* is singular
2. ENDING: dative masculine singular → **-em**

Von welchem Film sprecht ihr?

CAREFUL—The word *what* is not always an interrogative adjective. It can also be an interrogative pronoun (see *What is an Interrogative Pronoun?*, p. 95). When it is a pronoun, *what* is not followed by a noun.

What is on the table?   80
|
interrogative pronoun
Was ist auf dem Tisch?

It is important that you distinguish interrogative adjectives from interrogative pronouns because, in German, different words are used and they follow different rules.

— *REVIEW* —

I. Underline the interrogative adjective in the following sentences.
- Circle the noun about which the question is being asked.

1. What newspaper do you read?

2. Which record did you buy?

3. Do you know what homework is due?

4. Which hotel are you staying at?

5. Which game did you see?

II. Rewrite these questions in English to eliminate the dangling prepositions.

1. Which topic did you write about?

_____

2. Which people did you talk to?

_____

WHAT IS A DESCRIPTIVE ADJECTIVE?

1   A DESCRIPTIVE ADJECTIVE is a word that indicates a quality of a
noun or pronoun. As the name implies, it
describes the noun or pronoun.

The book is *interesting.*
noun   descriptive
described adjective

IN ENGLISH ────────────────────────────────

A descriptive adjective does not change form, regardless of
10 the noun or pronoun it modifies.

The students are *intelligent.*
She is an *intelligent* person.

The form of the adjective *intelligent* remains the same
although the persons described are different in number *(students* is plural and *person* is singular).

Descriptive adjectives are divided into two groups depending on how they are connected to the noun they modify.

1. A PREDICATE ADJECTIVE is connected to the noun it
20 describes, always the subject of the sentence, by LINKING
VERBS such as *to be, to feel, to look.* (See *What is a Predicate
Noun?,* p. 39.)

The children are *good.*
noun   linking predicate
described verb   adjective

The house looks *small.*
noun   linking predicate
described verb   adjective

30 2. An ATTRIBUTIVE ADJECTIVE is connected directly to the
noun it describes and always precedes it.

The *good* children were praised.
attributive noun
adjective   described

The family lives in a *small* house.
attributive noun
adjective   described

IN GERMAN ———————————————— 40

As in English, descriptive adjectives can be identified as predicate or attributive adjectives according to the way they are connected to the noun they describe. While predicate adjectives do not take special endings in German, attributive adjectives do.

PREDICATE ADJECTIVES—Predicate adjectives have the same form as the dictionary entry for the adjective, regardless of the gender and number of the nouns or pronouns they modify. 50

The children are small.
Die Kinder sind **klein**.
 |
 neuter plural

The house is small.
Das Haus ist **klein**.
 |
 neuter singular

ATTRIBUTIVE ADJECTIVES—There are three different sets of endings for attributive adjectives depending on the type of article, if any, which precedes the noun described: **WEAK ENDINGS, STRONG ENDINGS**, and **MIXED ENDINGS**. 60

You should have no problem selecting the appropriate endings in your textbook, if you follow these steps:

1. **NOUN DESCRIBED**—Identify the noun described by the attributive adjective.
2. **ARTICLE**—Look for the type of article, or lack of article, preceding the noun described. This will tell you from which of the three sets of endings you should choose.
   - if the noun described is a **der**-word, that is a noun preceded by a definite article, the attributive adjective takes **WEAK ENDINGS**. These are the most common 70 adjective endings: **der** gelbe Fisch, **die** bunten Autos.
   - if the noun described is not preceded by any article, the attributive adjective takes **STRONG ENDINGS**: gelber Fisch, blaues Auto.
   - if the noun described is an **ein**-word, that is a noun preceded by an indefinite article, the attributive adjective takes **MIXED ENDINGS**, some cases having strong endings and other cases having weak endings: **ein** gelber Fisch, **ein** blaues Auto. 80
3. **GENDER**—What is the gender of the noun described: masculine, feminine, or neuter?

4. NUMBER—Is the noun described singular or plural?
5. CASE—What is the case of the noun described: nominative, accusative, dative, or genitive?
5. SELECTION—Look under the appropriate set of endings found under step one for the ending which corresponds to the gender, number, and case of the noun described.

To show you the variety of possible endings, below are the three sets of endings of attributive adjectives in the nominative case: **Fisch** *(fish)*, masculine; **Blume** *(flower)*, feminine; **Auto** *(car)* neuter.

AFTER DER-WORD	AFTER EIN-WORD	NO ARTICLE
der gelbe Fisch	ein gelber Fisch	gelber Fisch
the yellow fish	*a yellow fish*	*yellow fish*
die rote Blume	eine rote Blume	rote Blume
the red flower	*a red flower*	*red flower*
das blaue Auto	ein blaues Auto	blaues Auto
the blue car	*a blue car*	*blue car*
die bunten Autos		bunte Autos
the colorful car		*colorful cars*

Your textbook will give you charts of the various endings for attributive adjectives.

— REVIEW —

Underline the adjective in the following sentences.
■ Indicate which set of adjective endings you need in German: after **der**-word (AD), after **ein**-word (AE), no article (NA):

1. The child plays in front of a red door.   AD   AE   NA
2. The fresh juice tastes good.   AD   AE   NA
3. Old shoes are comfortable.   AD   AE   NA
4. I'll have the large pizza.   AD   AE   NA
5. That's a friendly face.   AD   AE   NA

WHAT IS MEANT BY COMPARISON
OF ADJECTIVES?

The term **COMPARISON OF ADJECTIVES** is used when two or more [1] persons or things have the same quality (height, size, color, any characteristic) indicated by a descriptive adjective and we want to show which of these persons or things has a greater, lesser, or equal degree of that quality.

comparison of adjectives

Paul is *tall* but Mary is *taller*.

adjective   adjective
modifies *Paul*   modifies *Mary*

> Both nouns, *Paul* and *Mary*, have the same quality indicated [10] by the adjective *tall,* and we want to show that Mary has a greater degree of that quality (i.e., she is *taller* than Paul).

In English and in German, the quality of a person or thing can be compared with the same quality in another person or thing. The comparison can indicate that one has the same or a lesser amount of that quality, a greater amount of that quality, or the highest degree of that quality.

────────────── **COMPARATIVE** ──────────────

When two people or things share a quality, the comparative, [20] or comparison of **GREATER DEGREE,** is used to show that one has more of that quality than the other.

IN ENGLISH

The comparative of **GREATER DEGREE** (more) is formed differently depending on the length of the adjective being compared.

- short adjective + *-er* + ***than***

  Paul is tall*er than* Mary.
  Susan is young*er than* her sister.

[30]

- ***more*** + longer adjective + ***than***

  Mary is *more* intelligent *than* John.
  His car is *more* expensive *than* ours.

The comparison of **EQUAL DEGREE** (same) is formed as follows: ***as*** + adjective + ***as.***

> Robert is *as* tall *as* Mary.
> My car is *as* expensive *as* his car.

The comparison of LESSER DEGREE (less) is formed as follows: *not as* + adjective *as*, or *less* + adjective + *than*.

> Mary is *not as* tall *as* Paul.
> My car is *less* expensive *than* your car.

IN GERMAN

Unlike English, the comparison of GREATER DEGREE (more), does not depend on the length of the adjective. The comparative is always formed by adding -er to the stem of the adjective. The adjective endings are different for predicate and attributive adjectives (see p. 112).

PREDICATE ADJECTIVE—No ending is added after the comparative -er.

> Maria ist jünger als ihr Bruder.
> predicate adjective -er
> *Maria is younger than her brother*

> Das Buch ist interessanter als der Film.
> predicate adjective -er
> *The book is more interesting than the film.*

ATTRIBUTIVE ADJECTIVE—Add the appropriate adjective ending after the comparative -er. Consult your textbook for three sets of endings: weak, strong, and mixed. (see p. 113).

> Ich kenne das jüngere Mädchen nicht.
> attributive adjective -er + weak ending
> *I don't know the younger girl.*

> Das ist ein interessanterer Film.
> attributive adjective -er + strong ending
> *That is a more interesting film.*

As in English, the comparison of equal degree and of lesser degree are formed with set phrases:

The comparison of EQUAL DEGREE (same) is formed as follows: **so** *(as)* + adjective + **wie** *(as)*.

> Robert ist **so gross wie** Mary.
> *Robert is as tall as Mary.*

> Mein Auto ist **so teuer wie** sein Auto.
> *My car is as expensive as his car.*

The comparison of LESSER DEGREE (less) is formed as follows: **nicht so** *(less)* + adjective + **wie** *(than)*.

Mary ist **nicht so gross wie** Paul.
*Mary is **not as tall as** Paul.*

Sally ist **nicht so jung wie** Susan.
*Sally is **not as young as** Susan.*

───────────── **SUPERLATIVE** ─────────────

The superlative form is used to stress the highest degree of a quality.

IN ENGLISH

The superlative of highest degree is formed in one of two ways:

1. *the* + short adjective + *-est*

> Mary is *the* calm*est* in the family.
> My car is *the* saf*est* on the market.

2. *the most* + long adjective

> That argument was *the most* convincing.
> This book is *the most* interesting of all.

IN GERMAN

The superlative degree of the adjective is formed by adding -st to the adjective stem (-est if the adjective stem ends in -d, -t, -z, -s, or -ß). The structure and the ending of the superlative form will be different if it is a predicate or attributive adjective.

PREDICATE ADJECTIVE—The superlative is the two-word form: **am** + adjective + **-st-** (or **-est-**) + **-en.**

> Inge ist **am kleinsten.**
> *Inge is **the smallest.***

> Dieses Buch ist **am neuesten.**
> *This book is **the newest.***

> Im Winter ist das Wetter **am kältesten.**
> *In winter the weather is **(the) coldest.***

ATTRIBUTIVE ADJECTIVE—The superlative is preceded by a definite article (**der, die,** or **das**) plus the weak ending that corresponds to the case, number, and gender of the noun it modifies: article + adjective + **-st-** (or **-est-**) + weak ending (see p. 113).

120
Inge ist **das** kleinste Mädchen in der Schule.
*Inge is **the** smallest girl in the school.*

Hier ist **die** neueste Musik.
*Here is **the** newest music.*

CAREFUL—In English and in German there are several adjectives that form the comparative and the superlative in irregular ways:

good	gut	*much*	viel
better	besser	*more*	mehr
best	am besten	*most*	am meisten

130
You will find a list of irregular comparative and superlative forms in your German textbook which you will have to memorize.

— *REVIEW* —

Using the words given, write sentences with comparative adjectives. The various degrees of comparison are indicated as follows:

++   superlative
+   greater degree
=   equal degree
-      lesser degree

1. The teacher is / (+) old / the students.

_____

2. This student is / (=) intelligent / that one.

_____

3. Kathy is / (-) tall / Molly.

_____

4. This movie is / (++) good / this season.

_____

5. Today is / (++) hot / day on record.

_____

WHAT ARE REFLEXIVE PRONOUNS AND VERBS?

A **REFLEXIVE VERB** is a verb which is accompanied   1
by a pronoun, called a **REFLEXIVE PRONOUN**, that serves
"to reflect" the action of the verb back to the subject.

subject reflexive pronoun → the same person

She *cut herself* with the knife.

reflexive verb

IN ENGLISH ——————————————————————

Many regular verbs can take on a reflexive meaning by   10
adding a reflexive pronoun.

The child *dresses* the doll.

regular verb

The child *dresses herself.*

verb + reflexive pronoun

Reflexive pronouns end with *-self* in the singular and
-selves in the plural.

	SUBJECT PRONOUN	REFLEXIVE PRONOUN
SINGULAR			20
1ˢᵀ PERSON	I	myself
2ᴺᴰ PERSON	you	yourself
3ᴿᴰ PERSON	he	himself
	she	herself
	it	itself
PLURAL		
1ˢᵀ PERSON	we	ourselves
2ᴺᴰ PERSON	you	yourselves
3ᴿᴰ PERSON	they	themselves

As the subject changes so does the reflexive pronoun,
because they both refer to the same person or object.

I cut *myself.*
John and Mary blamed *themselves* for the accident.

Although the subject pronoun *you* is the same for the singular and plural, there is a difference in the reflexive pronouns: *yourself* (singular) is used when you are speaking to one person and *yourselves* (plural) is used when you are speaking to more than one.

> *Paul*, did *you* make *yourself* a sandwich?
> *Children*, make sure *you* wash *yourselves* properly.

Reflexive verbs can be in any tense: *I wash myself, I washed myself, I will wash myself*, etc.

A reflexive pronoun can have various functions in a sentence, such as direct object, indirect object, and object of a preposition (see *What are Objects?*, p. 52).

IN GERMAN

As in English, German reflexive verbs are formed with a verb and a reflexive pronoun. As you learn new vocabulary, you will need to memorize which German verbs are reflexive, that is, which ones require the reflexive pronoun as part of the whole verb.

A number of verbs can be used with or without reflexive pronouns, and sometimes verbs have a different meaning when they are reflexive. Your German textbook will introduce you to these verbs.

REFLEXIVE PRONOUNS

As in English, there are reflexive pronouns in German for each of the different personal pronouns (1st, 2nd, and 3rd persons, singular and plural). Unlike English, the German reflexive pronouns have both an accusative form and a dative form. Depending on the verb or the preposition, you will have to choose either the accusative or the dative reflexive pronoun.

Here are the German subject pronouns and the corresponding reflexive pronouns:

SUBJECT	REFLEXIVE		
NOMINATIVE	ACCUSATIVE	DATIVE	
ich	mich	mir	*myself*
du	dich	dir	*yourself*
er			
sie	sich	sich	*himself, herself,*
es			*itself*
wir	uns	uns	*ourselves*
ihr	euch	euch	*yourselves*
sie	sich	sich	*themselves*
Sie	sich	sich	*yourself, yourselves*

A reflexive pronoun in German can function as different types of objects: [80]

- as direct or indirect object of the verb

  *I cut **myself** with the knife.*
  direct object of *cut*
  I cut *whom*? Myself → direct object
  Ich habe **mich** mit dem Messer geschnitten.
  accusative object of **geschnitten** *(to cut)*

  *You should write **yourself** a note.* [90]
  indirect object of *write*
  You should write *to whom*? To yourself → indirect object
  Du solltest **dir** einen Zettel schreiben.
  dative object of **schreiben** *(to write)*

- as object of a preposition

  *He thinks only of **himself**.*
  object of preposition *of*
  Remember: *to think of* → **denken an** + accusative
  Er denkt nur an **sich**. [100]
  accusative object of **denken an**

  *You talk about **yourself** too much.*
  object of preposition *about*
  Remember: *to talk about* → **reden von** + dative
  Du redest zuviel von **dir**.
  dative object of **von**

─────────── **REFLEXIVE VERBS** ───────────

There are some German verbs that must have reflexive pronouns to complete their meaning. These verbs are called **REFLEXIVE VERBS**. The English equivalents of these verbs do not have reflexive pronouns. [110]

sich erholen	*to recover*
sich befinden	*to be located*
sich verlieben	*to fall in love*

German reflexive verbs are listed in the dictionary with the infinitive + the third person reflexive pronoun, **sich**.

Look at the conjugation of **sich erholen** *(to recover)* which takes an accusative object. [120]

ich	erhole	mich	*I recover*
du	erholst	dich	*you recover*
er	erholt	sich	*he, it recovers*
sie	erholt	sich	*she, it recovers*
es	erholt	sich	*it recovers*
wir	erholen	uns	*we recover*
ihr	erholt	euch	*you recover*
sie	erholen	sich	*they recover*
Sie	erholen	sich	*you recover*

Reflexive verbs can be conjugated in all tenses. The subject pronoun and reflexive pronoun remain the same regardless of the verb tense; only the verb form changes: *du* erholst *dich* (present), *du* wirst *dich* erholen (future), *du* hast *dich* erholt (perfect).

CAREFUL—When German reflexive pronouns are used as objects of verbs and as objects of prepositions, you will need to pay attention to the case required. Remember that the case of the reflexive pronoun depends on its function in the German sentence, not the English sentence. Pay special attention to verbs that take a direct object in English, but require the dative case in German.

> *I can't help **myself**.*
> |
>   direct object of *help*
>
>   Remember: *to help* → **helfen** + dative
> Ich kann **mir** nicht helfen.
> |
>   dative object of **helfen**

— *REVIEW* —

I. Fill in the proper reflexive pronoun in English.

1. Ruby, you should feel free to make _____ at home.

2. We fixed the car _____.

3. He picked everything up by _____.

4. She wanted some time to _____.

5. I wish I'd thought of that _____.

6. Maura and Steve, you should get _____ ready.

II. Using the sample conjugation on p. 122, fill in the accusative reflexive pronouns of the reflexive verb **sich freuen über** *(to be happy about something).*

ich freue   _____

du freust   _____

er, sie, es freut   _____

wir freuen   _____

ihr freut   _____

sie, Sie freuen   _____

CHAPTER

WHAT IS AN ADVERB?

An **ADVERB** is a word that describes a verb, an adjective, or another adverb. It indicates manner, degree, time, place.

Mary drives *well*.
| |
verb adverb

The house is *very* big.
| |
adverb adjective

The girl ran *too quickly*.
| |
adverb adverb

IN ENGLISH ───────────────────────────────

There are different types of adverbs:

- an **ADVERB OF MANNER** answers the question *how?* Adverbs of manner are the most common and they are easy to recognize because they end with **-ly**.

  Mary sings *beautifully*.

  Beautifully describes the verb *sings*; it tells you how Mary sings.

- an **ADVERB OF DEGREE** answers the question *how much?*

  Paul did *well* on the exam.

- an **ADVERB OF TIME** answers the question *when?*

  He will come *soon*.

- an **ADVERB OF PLACE** answers the question *where?*

  The children were left *behind*.

A few adverbs in English are identical in form to the corresponding adjectives (see *What is an Adjective?*, p. 103):

ADVERB	ADJECTIVE
The guests came *late*.	We greeted the *late* guests.
Don't drive so *fast*.	*Fast* drivers cause accidents.
She works very *hard*.	This is *hard* work.

CAREFUL—Remember that in English *good* is an adjective since it modifies a noun and *well* is an adverb since it modifies a verb.

The student writes *good* English.
Good modifies the noun *English;* it is an adjective.

The student writes *well.*
Well modifies the verb *writes;* it is an adverb.

40

IN GERMAN ————————————————————

As in English, there are words that function only as adverbs.

Das Haus ist **sehr** groß.
*The house is **very** big.*

Er kommt **bald.**
*He is coming **soon.***

Unlike English, however, many German adverbs have the same form as their corresponding adjectives.

50

ADVERB	ADJECTIVE
Du hast das **gut** gemacht.	Dieses Buch ist **gut.**
*You did that **well.***	*This book is **good.***
Sie singen **schön.**	Das Lied ist **schön.**
*They sing **beautifully.***	*The song is **beautiful.***
Wir fahren **schnell.**	Der Wagen ist **schnell.**
*We drive **fast.***	*The car is **fast.***

— **REVIEW** —

Circle the adverbs in the sentences below.
■ Draw an arrow from each adverb to the word it modifies.

1. The guests arrived early.

2. They were too tired to go out.

3. David learned the lesson really quickly.

4. We stayed here.

5. Meg is a good student who speaks German very well.

CHAPTER

39

WHAT IS A PREPOSITION?

¹ A **PREPOSITION** is a word that shows the relationship of one word (usually a noun or pronoun) to another word (usually another noun or pronoun) in the sentence.

prepositional phrase

Paul has an appointment *after* school.

preposition   object of preposition

¹⁰ The noun or pronoun following the preposition is called the **OBJECT OF THE PREPOSITION.** The preposition plus its object is called a **PREPOSITIONAL PHRASE.**

IN ENGLISH ───────────────────────────

Prepositions normally indicate location, direction, time or manner.

- prepositions showing location or position

  Michael was *in* the car.
  Anna is sitting *behind* you.

- prepositions showing direction

²⁰
  We went *to* school.
  The students came directly *from* class.

- prepositions showing time and date

  Many Germans vacation *in* August.
  Their son will be home *at* Christmas.
  I'm meeting him *before* 4:30 today.

- prepositions showing manner

  He writes *with* a pen.
  They left *without* us.

³⁰ Other frequently used prepositions are: *during, since, between, of, about.* Some English prepositions are made up of more than a single word: *because of, in front of, instead of, due to, in spite of, on account of.*

IN GERMAN ───────────────────────────

As in English, prepositions never change form. You will have to memorize them as vocabulary, paying special attention to their meaning and use. Unlike English, however, the noun or pronoun object of the preposition will

be in the accusative, dative, or genitive case depending on
the preposition. As you memorize each German preposition, be sure to memorize the case that must follow it.
(See p. 56 in *What are Objects?*, and *What are Object of
Preposition Pronouns?*, p. 131).

Below are examples of various prepositions, each requiring a different case.

- **durch** *(through)* → accusative object

  Der Hund läuft **durch** die Tür.

         |

      accusative

  *The dog is running **through** the door.*

- **bei** *(with)* → dative object

  Er wohnt **bei** seiner Tante.

       |

     dative

  *He lives **with** his aunt.*

- **trotz** *(in spite of)* → genitive object

  Trotz des Regens machten wir einen Spaziergang.

      |

    genitive

  *In **spite** of the rain we took a walk.*

──────────────── **TWO-WAY PREPOSITIONS** ────────────────

German also has a group of prepositions called TWO-WAY
PREPOSITIONS, so called because they can be followed by
either an accusative object or a dative object depending
on the way the preposition is used.

1. When used with a verb expressing motion in a particular direction, the preposition is followed by an
   accusative object.

   *We are driving **into** town tomorrow.*
   Wir fahren morgen **in** die Stadt.

            |

         accusative

   *He lays the book **on** the table.*
   Er legt das Buch **auf** den Tisch.

           |

        accusative

2. When used with a verb expressing location or direc-
   tionless motion, the preposition is followed by a dative
   object.

   *Do you live **in** the city?*
   Wohnt ihr **in** der Stadt?

         |

       dative

*The book lies **on** the table.*
Das Buch liegt **auf** dem Tisch.
dative

CAREFUL—Prepositions are tricky, because every language uses prepositions differently. Do not assume that the same preposition is used in German as in English, or even that a preposition will be needed in German when you must use one in English and vice versa.

ENGLISH	GERMAN
PREPOSITION	NO PREPOSITION
to look *for*	suchen
to look *at*	betrachten
NO PREPOSITION	PREPOSITION
to answer	antworten **auf**

CHANGE OF PREPOSITION	
to protect *from*	schützen **vor** *(before)*
to wait *for*	warten **auf** *(on)*
to die *of*	sterben **an** *(at)*

A dictionary will usually give you the verb plus the preposition which follows it, when one is required. Do not translate an English verb + preposition word-for-word. For example, when you consult the dictionary to find the German equivalent of *to talk about*, do not stop at the first entry for *talk* (which is **sprechen**) and then add the German equivalent of the preposition *about*. Continue searching for the specific meaning *talk about*, which corresponds to the verb **sprechen** with the preposition **über** (meaning *over* or *above*).

*We are talking **about** politics.*
Wir sprechen **über** Politik.

On the other hand, when looking up a verb such as *to pay for something*, notice that the German equivalent **bezahlen** is used without a preposition.

*We paid **for** the meal.*
Wir bezahlten das Essen.

———————— **POSITION OF A PREPOSITION** ————————

IN ENGLISH

The position of a preposition in an English sentence is much more variable than in a German sentence. In spoken English, prepositions tend to be at the end of the sen-

tence, far from its object; this is called a DANGLING PREPOSI-
TION. In formal English, the prepositions are placed within
the sentence or at the beginning of a question. Here are
some examples.

SPOKEN ENGLISH $\rightarrow$	FORMAL ENGLISH
Here is the man I talk *to*.	Here is the man *to whom* I talk.
Who(m) are you working *with*?	*With whom* are you working?
That's the teacher I'm talking *about*.	That's the teacher *about whom* I'm talking.

IN GERMAN

Prepositions are placed the same way as in formal English,
that is, within the sentence or at the beginning of a question (see also danging prepositions, p. 98 and p. 128).
Nearly all German prepositions come right before their
objects. Your textbook will indicate the few prepositions
that must or can follow their objects.

CAREFUL—In German sentences, do not mistake separable
prefixes which are placed at the end of sentences for
prepositions (see *What are Prefixes and Suffixes?*, p. 28).

Wer **kommt mit?**
Who is coming along?

Das **kommt** manchmal **vor.**
That happens sometimes.

Der Zug **hält** in München **an.**
The train stops in Munich.

You will easily recognize **mit**, **vor**, and **an** as separable
prefixes and not prepositions if you remember that a
preposition is never separated from its object. In the sentences above, **mit**, **vor**, and **an** are the separable prefixes
of the verbs **mitkommen** *(to come along)*, **vorkommen** *(to
happen)*, and **anhalten** *(to stop)*.

— *REVIEW* —

I. Circle the prepositions in the following sentences.

1. A mouse darted behind the table.

2. The letter was hidden under the papers.

3. We met at the museum in Stuttgart.

4. On Saturday let's look around the city.

II. Restructure the dangling prepositions in the following sentences so that the structure in English will parallel the structure of a German sentence.

1. I can't tell what they're laughing about.

_____

2. Who are you doing that for?

_____

40

WHAT ARE OBJECT OF PREPOSITION PRONOUNS?

Object pronouns are also used as [1]
OBJECTS OF A PREPOSITION.

They went out with *me*.
|
object of preposition *with*

IN ENGLISH ————————————————————
The same forms of object pronouns are used for direct objects, indirect objects and objects of a preposition (see *What are Direct and Indirect Object Pronouns?*, p. 58). [10]

IN GERMAN ————————————————————
The objects of prepositions in German can be in the accusative, dative, or genitive case. Normally we replace a noun object with a pronoun only if the noun replaced refers to a person. A different construction is used when the pronoun refers to a thing or idea. Let us look at the two types of constructions.

———————————— **"PERSON"** ————————————
When the pronoun object of a preposition refers to a person or an animal, follow the steps you have already learned to [20] choose the appropriate personal pronoun (see p. 20):

1. ANTECEDENT—Find the noun replaced.
2. GENDER—Determine the gender of the antecedent.
3. CASE—Identify the case required by the preposition.
4. SELECTION—Select the appropriate pronoun form from the chart on p. 59.

Below are examples showing how to analyze sentences that have a pronoun referring to a person as the object of a preposition. [30]

Is Molly buying something for her brother?
*Yes, she is buying something for **him**.*
    1. ANTECEDENT: brother
    2. GENDER: **der Bruder** *(brother)* is masculine.
    3. CASE: **für** takes an accusative object
    4. SELECTION: masculine accusative → **ihn**
Kauft Molly etwas für ihren Bruder?
Ja, sie kauft etwas **für ihn.**

Did John talk about his sister?
*No, he did not talk **about her**.*
　1. ANTECEDENT: sister
　2. GENDER: **die Schwester** *(sister)* is feminine.
　3. CASE: **von** takes a dative object
　4. SELECTION: feminine dative → **ihr**
Sprach John von seiner Schwester?
Nein, er sprach nicht **von ihr**.

────────────────── **"THING"** ──────────────────

In German, pronouns are not normally used as the object of a preposition when the antecedent is a thing or an idea. Unlike English, which uses the construction preposition + *it* or preposition + *them*, you will need to use a special German construction called the "DA-COMPOUND." This construction takes the place of a preposition + a pronoun. It is formed by adding the prefix **da-** to the preposition, or **dar-** if the preposition begins with a vowel.

Let us look at some examples:

*Are you thinking **about the price**? Don't think **about it**.*
Denken Sie **an den Preis**? Denken Sie nicht **daran**!

　　preposition　　noun　　　　da-construction:
　　　　　　　　　(a thing)　　　**da + r +** preposition **an**

*Does Beth talk **about her courses**? Yes, she does talk **about them**.*
Spricht Beth **von ihren Kursen**? Ja, sie spricht **davon**.

　　preposition　　noun　　　　da-construction:
　　　　　　　　　(a thing)　　　**da +** preposition **von**

Your German textbook will discuss this construction and its use in greater detail.

────────────────── **— REVIEW —** ──────────────────

I. The following English sentences contain prepositions and their objects written in italics.
- Circle italicized nouns referring to persons.
- Underline italicized nouns referring to things.
- Indicate the type of construction you must use in German: preposition + personal pronoun (PP) or **da**-compound (**da**-C).

1. We're waiting *for Greg*.　　　　　　　PP　　　**da**-C

2. Thank you *for the present*!　　　　　PP　　　**da**-C

3. I wrote *to Emily*.　　　　　　　　　　PP　　　**da**-C

4. We're looking forward *to the vacation*.　PP　　　**da**-C

WHAT IS A CONJUNCTION?

A **CONJUNCTION** is a word that links two
or more words or groups of words.

> He had to choose between good *and* evil.
> |
> conjunction

> They left *because* they were bored.
> |
> conjunction

IN ENGLISH

There are two kinds of conjunctions: coordinating and
subordinating.

- a **COORDINATING CONJUNCTION** joins words, phrases (groups
  of words without a verb), and clauses (groups of words
  with a verb) that are equal; it *coordinates* elements of
  equal rank. The major coordinating conjunctions are
  and, but, or, nor, for, and *yet.*

> good *or* evil
> | |
> word word

> over the river *and* through the woods
> |_____| |_____|
> phrase   phrase

> They invited us *but* we couldn't go.
> |_____| |_____|
> clause   clause

In the last example, each of the two clauses, "they
invited us" and "we couldn't go," expresses a complete
thought; each clause is, therefore, a complete sentence
which could stand alone. When a clause expresses a
complete sentence it is called a **MAIN CLAUSE**. In the
above sentence, the coordinating conjunction *but* links
two main clauses.

- a **SUBORDINATING CONJUNCTION** joins a main clause to
  a dependent clause; it *subordinates* one clause to another. A **DEPENDENT CLAUSE** does not express a complete
  thought; it is, therefore, not a complete sentence and
  cannot stand alone. There are various types of dependent clauses. A clause introduced by a subordinating
  conjunction is called a **SUBORDINATE CLAUSE**. Typical sub-

ordinating conjunctions are *before, after, since, although, because, if, unless, so that, while, that,* and *when.*

subordinate clause   main clause

Although we were invited, we didn't go.

subordinating
conjunction

main clause   subordinate clause

They left *because* they were bored.

subordinating
conjunction

main clause subordinate clause

He said *that* he was tired.

subordinating
conjunction

In the above examples, "although we were invited," "because they were bored," and "that he was tired," are all subordinate clauses. They are not complete sentences and each is introduced by a subordinating conjunction.

Notice that the subordinate clause may come either at the beginning of the sentence or after the main clause.

IN GERMAN ─────────────────────────────────

Conjunctions must be memorized as vocabulary items. Like adverbs and prepositions, conjunctions are invariable (i.e., they never change their form). Your German textbook will explain special rules of usage for conjunctions.

The major coordinating conjunctions are **und** *(and),* **oder** *(or),* **aber** *(but),* **sondern** *(but, on the contrary),* and **denn** *(for).* Typical subordinating conjunctions include **obgleich** *(although),* **obwohl** *(although),* **weil** *(because),* **wenn** *(if, whenever),* **damit** *(in order that),* **dass** *(that),* and **während** *(while).*

───────── **PREPOSITION OR CONJUNCTION?** ─────────

IN ENGLISH

Some words function as both prepositions and subordinating conjunctions, for example, *before* and *after.* We can identify the word's function by determining whether or not it introduces a clause.

If the word in question introduces a clause, it is a subordinating conjunction. The clause will contain a subject and a verb (see *What is a Sentence?,* p. 47).

We left *before* the intermission began.
         | |_____|
       subordinating   subject + verb = clause
       conjunction

After the concert was over, we ate ice cream.
  | |_____|
subordinating subject + verb = clause
conjunction

If the word in question does not introduce a clause, it is a preposition. The preposition is followed by an object, but no verb.

We left *before* the intermission.
         | |
     preposition   object of preposition

After the concert we ate ice cream.
  | |
preposition object of preposition

IN GERMAN

It is important for you to establish whether a word is a preposition or a conjunction because in German you will use different words and apply different rules of grammar depending on the part of speech.

ENGLISH PREPOSITION AND CONJUNCTION	GERMAN	
	PREPOSITION	CONJUNCTION
before	vor	bevor
after	nach	nachdem

Let us look at some examples using these different parts of speech.

■ *before* and *after* as prepositions

> *We left **before** the intermission.*
> Wir sind **vor** der Pause weggegangen.

> *After the concert we ate ice cream.*
> **Nach** dem Konzert haben wir Eis gegessen.

■ *before* and *after* as conjunctions

> *We left **before** the intermission began.*
> Wir sind weggegangen, **bevor** die Pause anfing.

> *After the concert was over, we ate ice cream.*
> **Nachdem** das Konzert vorbei war, aßen wir Eis.

Knowing the part of speech of the new words that you learn will help you choose the correct word in German and apply the proper rules of grammar.

— REVIEW —

I. Circle the coordinating and subordinating conjunctions.

1. We can have a picnic unless it starts raining.

2. She stopped studying because she was too tired.

3. He forgot his watch, but he remembered his passport.

II. Underline the prepositions in the following sentences.
- Box in the conjunctions.

1. Since the weather turned cold, we've stayed inside.

2. I've know him since high school.

3. We were home before midnight.

4. Before we leave, we'd better say goodbye.

WHAT IS A RELATIVE PRONOUN?

A RELATIVE PRONOUN is a word used at the beginning of a clause which gives additional information about someone or something previously mentioned.

clause
additional information about *the book*

I'm reading the book *that* the teacher recommended.

A relative pronoun serves two purposes:

1. As a pronoun it stands for a noun previously mentioned. The noun to which it refers is called the ANTECEDENT.

This is the boy *who* broke the window.

antecedent of the relative pronoun *who*

2. It introduces a SUBORDINATE CLAUSE; that is, a group of words having a subject and a verb which cannot stand alone because it does not express a complete thought. A subordinate clause is dependent on a MAIN CLAUSE; that is, another group of words having a subject and a verb which can stand alone as a complete sentence.

main clause   subordinate clause

Here comes the boy *who broke the window.*

verb   subject verb

A subordinate clause that starts with a relative pronoun is also called a RELATIVE CLAUSE. In the example above, the relative clause starts with the relative pronoun *who* and gives us additional information about the antecedent *boy.*

Relative clauses are very common. We use them in everyday speech without giving much thought as to how we construct them. The relative pronoun allows us to combine two thoughts which have a common element into a single sentence.

——— COMBINING SENTENCES WITH A RELATIVE PRONOUN ———

When sentences are combined with a relative pronoun, the relative pronoun can have different functions in the relative clause. It can be the subject, the direct object, the indirect object, or the object of a preposition.

Let us look at some examples of how sentences are combined.

- relative pronoun as a subject

> SENTENCE A   The students passed the exam.
> SENTENCE B   They studied.

1. COMMON ELEMENT—Identify the element the two sentences have in common.

> Both *the students* and *they* refer to the same persons.

2. ANTECEDENT—The common element in the first sentence will be the antecedent of the relative pronoun and will remain unchanged. The common element in the second sentence will be replaced by a relative pronoun.

> *The students* is the antecedent and remains unchanged.
> *They* will be replaced by a relative pronoun.

3. FUNCTION—The relative pronoun in the relative clause has the same function as the word it replaces.

> *They* is the subject of *studied.* Therefore,
> the relative pronoun will be the subject of *studied.*

4. PERSON OR THING—Choose the relative pronoun according to whether its antecedent refers to a person or a thing.

> The antecedent *students* refers to persons.

5. SELECTION—Select the relative pronoun.

> *Who* or *that* is the subject relative pronoun
> referring to a person or persons.

6. RELATIVE CLAUSE—Place the relative pronoun at the beginning of the second sentence, thus forming a relative clause.

> *who* studied
> *that* studied

7. PLACEMENT—Place the relative clause right after its antecedent.

> COMBINED   The students *who* studied passed the exam.
> The students *that* studied passed the exam.
>   antecedent   relative clause

- relative pronoun as a direct object

  SENTENCE A This is the student.
  SENTENCE B I saw him.

  1. COMMON ELEMENT: *the student* and *him*
  2. ANTECEDENT: the student
  3. FUNCTION: *him* is the direct object
  4. PERSON OR THING: *the student* is a person
  5. SELECTION: *that* or *whom*
  6. RELATIVE CLAUSE: *that (whom)* I saw
  7. PLACEMENT: the student + *that (whom)* I saw

  COMBINED   This is the student *(that)* I saw.
               This is the student *(whom)* I saw.

               antecedent   relative clause

- relative pronoun as an indirect object

  SENTENCE A This is the student.
  SENTENCE B I spoke to him.

  1. COMMON ELEMENT: *the student* and *him*
  2. ANTECEDENT: the student
  3. FUNCTION: *him* is the indirect object
  4. PERSON OR THING: *the student* is a person
  5. SELECTION: *to whom*
  6. RELATIVE CLAUSE: *to whom* I spoke
  7. PLACEMENT: the student + *to whom* I spoke

  COMBINED   This is the student *to whom* I spoke.

               antecedent   relative clause

- relative pronoun as an object of a preposition

  SENTENCE A This is the student.
  SENTENCE B I spoke with him.

  1. COMMON ELEMENT: *the student* and *him*
  2. ANTECEDENT: the student
  3. FUNCTION: *him* is the object of the preposition *with*
  4. PERSON OR THING: *the student* is a person
  5. SELECTION: *whom*
  6. RELATIVE CLAUSE: *with whom* I spoke
  7. PLACEMENT: the student + *with whom* I spoke

  COMBINED   This is the student *with whom* I spoke.

               antecedent   relative clause

─────────── **SELECTION OF THE RELATIVE PRONOUN** ───────────

IN ENGLISH

In an English sentence, relative pronouns can sometimes be omitted.

The book I'm reading is interesting.
The book *that* I'm reading is interesting.

relative pronoun

The selection of a relative pronoun in English often depends not only on its function in the relative clause, but also on whether its antecedent is a "person" (human beings and animals) or a "thing" (objects and ideas).

IN GERMAN

The main difference between English and German relative pronouns is that relative pronouns must always be expressed in German sentences.

Unlike English, it does not matter whether the antecedent is a person or a thing; the same set of relative pronouns refers to both. What is important is the gender and number of the antecedent; this will determine the gender and number of the relative pronoun. Also, German relative pronouns have four different case forms: nominative, accusative, dative, and genitive, depending on the function of the pronoun in the relative clause (see *What is Meant by Case?*, p. 31). We shall look at each function separately. (Notice in the German sentences below that all relative clauses are separated by commas from the main clause.)

──────── **SUBJECT OF THE RELATIVE CLAUSE** ────────
(see *What is a Subject?*, p. 36)

IN ENGLISH

There are three relative pronouns that can be used as subjects of a relative clause, depending on whether the relative pronoun refers to a person or a thing. When it is the subject of a relative clause, a relative pronoun is never omitted.

PERSON—*Who* or *that* is used as subject of the relative clause.

relative clause

She is the only student *who* answered all the time.
She is the only student *that* answered all the time.

THING—*Which* or *that* is used as subject of the relative clause.

The movie *which* is so popular was filmed in Germany.
The movie *that* is so popular was filmed in Germany.

antecedent   relative pronoun
             subject of *is*

Notice that the relative pronoun subject is always followed by a verb.

IN GERMAN

Relative pronouns which are the subject of the relative clause are in the nominative case. The form used depends on the gender of the antecedent.

SINGULAR		
MASCULINE	der	
FEMININE	die	*who, that, which*
NEUTER	das	
PLURAL	die	

To choose the correct form,

1. ANTECEDENT—Find the antecedent. (Don't forget that the antecedent is always the noun that precedes the relative pronoun.)
2. NUMBER & GENDER—Determine the number and gender of the antecedent.
3. SELECTION—Select the corresponding form.

Here is an example.

> *The man **who** visited us was nice.*
>   1. ANTECEDENT: man
>   2. NUMBER & GENDER: **der Mann** *(the man)* is masculine singular
>   3. SELECTION: masculine singular nominative → **der**

Der Mann, **der** uns besuchte, war nett.

──────────── **OBJECT OF THE RELATIVE CLAUSE** ────────────
(see *What are Objects?*, p. 52)

IN ENGLISH

There are three relative pronouns that can be used as objects of a relative clause, depending on whether the relative pronoun refers to a person or a thing. When it is the object of a relative clause, a relative pronoun is often omitted.

PERSON—When the antecedent is a person, ***whom*** or ***that*** is used as the object of a relative clause.

■ as a direct object

> This is the student *(whom)* I saw yesterday.
> This is the student *(that)* I saw yesterday.

■ as an indirect object

> Mary is the person *to whom* he gave the present.

- as an object of a preposition

> Mary is the person *with whom* he went out.

THING—When the antecedent is a thing, **which** or **that** is used as the object of a relative clause.

210
- as a direct object

> This is the book *(which)* Peter bought.
> This is the book *(that)* Peter bought.

- as an indirect object

> Here is the library *to which* he gave the book.

- as an object of a preposition

> Here is the library *about which* I was speaking.

CAREFUL—It can be difficult to identify the function of
220
relative pronouns as objects in English. Even when they are not omitted, they are often separated from the preposition of which they are the object. When a preposition is separated from its object and placed at the end of a sentence, it is called a DANGLING PREPOSITION (see p. 98).

> Here is the student *(that)* I was speaking *with*.
> Here is the library *(that)* he gave the book *to*.

English sentences which have omitted the relative pronoun or which have dangling prepositions have to be restructured in order to restore the relative pronoun and
230
establish its function. To restructure the English sentences, follow these steps.

1. ANTECEDENT—Identify the antecedent.
2. PREPOSITION—Place the preposition after the antecedent.
3. RESTORE THE PRONOUN—Add the relative pronoun *whom* or *which* after the preposition.

SPOKEN ENGLISH →	RESTRUCTURED
Here is the student	Here is the student
I was speaking *with*.	*with whom* I was speaking.
240 | | object of preposition *with* |

IN GERMAN

Relative pronouns which are the object of the relative clause are either in the accusative or dative case. The form used also depends on the gender of the antecedent.

	ACCUSATIVE	DATIVE	
SINGULAR			
MASCULINE	den	dem	
FEMININE	die	der	*who, that, which*
NEUTER	das	dem	
PLURAL	die	denen	

250

We have included the relative pronouns in the English sentences below to show you to what the German relative pronoun corresponds; however, we have put them between parentheses since they are often omitted in English.

- as a direct object or an object of a preposition requiring the accusative in German

    *Here is the student (**whom**) John saw last night.*
    Hier ist der Student, **den** John gestern Nacht sah.
    masc. sing. masc. sing. accusative

260

    *Here is the person I was waiting **for**.*
    RESTRUCTURE: *Here is the person **for whom** I was waiting.*
    Hier ist die Person, **auf die** ich wartete.
    fem. sing. | fem. sing. accusative
    preposition requiring accusative

- as an indirect object or an object of a preposition requiring the dative in German

270

    *Here is the student I was speaking **to**.*
    RESTRUCTURE: *Here is the student **to whom** I was speaking.*
    Hier ist der Student, zu **dem** ich sprach.
    masc. sing. masc. sing. dative

    *Here is the person I was speaking **with**.*
    RESTRUCTURE: *Here is the person **with whom** I was speaking.*
    Hier ist die Person, **mit der** ich sprach.
    fem. sing. | fem. sing. dative
    preposition requiring dative

280

——— RELATIVE PRONOUNS AS POSSESSIVE MODIFIERS ———

IN ENGLISH

The possessive modifier **whose** is a relative pronoun that does not change its form regardless of its function in the relative clause.

    Here are the people *whose* car was stolen.
    antecedent possessive modifying *car*

Look at the house *whose* roof was fixed.

antecedent   possessive modifying *roof*

IN GERMAN

The possessive modifier is always in the genitive case. The form used depends on the gender of the antecedent.

SINGULAR	GENITIVE	
MASCULINE	dessen	
FEMININE	deren	*whose*
NEUTER	dessen	
PLURAL	deren	

Let's look at an example.

*Hans, **whose** alarm clock was broken, overslept.*
1. ANTECEDENT: Hans
2. NUMBER & GENDER: *Hans* is masculine singular
3. SELECTION: **dessen**

Hans, **dessen** Wecker kaputt war, hat sich verschlafen.

─────────── **SUMMARY OF RELATIVE PRONOUNS** ───────────

Here is a chart you can use as reference:

FUNCTION IN RELATIVE CLAUSE	ANTECEDENT SINGULAR			ANTECEDENT PLURAL
	MASCULINE	FEMININE	NEUTER	
NOMINATIVE	der	die	das	die
ACCUSATIVE	den	die	das	die
DATIVE	dem	der	dem	denen
GENITIVE	dessen	deren	dessen	deren

────── **RELATIVE PRONOUNS WITHOUT ANTECEDENTS** ──────

There are relative pronouns that do not refer to a specific noun or pronoun. Instead, they refer to an antecedent which has not been expressed or to an entire idea.

IN ENGLISH

There are two relative pronouns that can be used without an antecedent: **what** and **which.**

What—does not refer to a specific noun or pronoun.

I don't know *what* happened.

no antecedent
subject

Here is *what* I read.   330
    |
    no antecedent
    direct object

Which—refers to an entire idea, not to a specific noun or pronoun.

She didn't do well, *which* is too bad.
                        |
    ANTECEDENT: the fact that she didn't do well
    subject of *is*

You speak many languages, *which* I envy.
                            | 340
    ANTECEDENT: the fact that you speak many languages
    direct object of *envy (I* is the subject)

IN GERMAN

When a relative pronoun does not have a specific antecedent, the pronoun **"was"** *(which, what)* is always used.

entire clause as antecedent   relative clause

Anna hat uns eingeladen, **was** wir nett gefunden haben.
*Anna invited us all, **which** we found nice.*

Your textbook may give you examples of other instances   350
which require the use of **was** as a relative pronoun.

— *REVIEW* —

I. Circle the antecedent of the relative pronoun in the following sentences.

- Identify the function of the relative pronoun: subject (S), direct object (DO), indirect object (IO), object of a preposition (OP), possessive modifier (PM).

1. I received the letter that you sent me.   S   DO   IO   OP   PM

2. Those are the people who speak German. S   DO   IO   OP   PM

3. The woman whom you met left today.   S   DO   IO   OP   PM

4. This is the book whose title I forgot.   S   DO   IO   OP   PM

5. Kit is the student about whom I spoke.   S   DO   IO   OP   PM

II. The common elements in the sentence below have been high-. lighted. Fill in the information requested to find the correct relative pronoun and write a new English sentence using a relative pronoun.

1. The *dog* is friendly. *It* lives next door.

   FUNCTION OF ELEMENT TO REPLACE:_____

   RELATIVE PRONOUN:_____

   COMBINED SENTENCE:_____

2. *The Smiths* left for Austria. You met *them* in Basel.

   FUNCTION OF ELEMENT TO REPLACE:_____

   RELATIVE PRONOUN:_____

   COMBINED SENTENCE:_____

3. The new student is German. You were asking about her.

   FUNCTION OF ELEMENT TO REPLACE:_____

   RELATIVE PRONOUN:_____

   COMBINED SENTENCE:_____

WHAT IS THE SUBJUNCTIVE?

The SUBJUNCTIVE is the mood of the verb used to express
    hypothetical or contrary-to-fact situations,
        in contrast to the indicative mood which
            is used to express facts. [1]

I wish Kathy *were* here.

hypothetical (Kathy is *not* here) → subjunctive

If Kathy *were* here, you could meet her.

contrary-to-fact (Kathy is *not* here) → subjunctive

Kathy *is* here. [10]

fact (Kathy is here) → indicative

IN ENGLISH ———————————————————

The subjunctive verb form is difficult to recognize because
it is spelled like other tenses of the verb: the dictionary
form and the simple past tense.

INDICATIVE	SUBJUNCTIVE
He *reads* a lot.	The course requires that he *read* a lot.
indicative present *to read*	subjunctive (same as dictionary form) [20]
I *am* in Boston right now.	I wish I *were* in Berlin.
indicative present *to be*	subjunctive (same as past tense)

The subjunctive occurs most commonly in three kinds of
sentences.

1. The subjunctive form of the verb *to be* (**were**) is used in
   the *if-clause* of contrary-to-fact sentences; the result
   clause uses *would* + infinitive.

   if-clause   result clause [30]

   If I *were* in Europe now, I would go to Berlin.

   subjunctive

       Contrary-to-fact: I am *not* in Europe.

   result clause   if clause

   John would run faster, if he *were* in shape.

   subjunctive

       Contrary-to-fact: John is *not* in shape.

2. The same subjunctive form *were* is used in the conclusion of a wish statement. The wish statement is in the
indicative.

I wish I *were* in Europe right now.
    | |
indicative subjunctive

John wishes he *were* in shape.
    | |
indicative subjunctive

3. The subjunctive form of any verb is used following
expressions that ask, urge, demand, request or express
necessity.

She asked that I *come* to see her.
request   subjunctive same as dictionary form

It is necessary that you *study* a lot.
demand   subjunctive same as dictionary form

IN GERMAN

As in English, German has two subjunctive forms, one
derived from the simple past of the verb and one derived
from the infinitive. In this section we will only discuss the
subjunctive derived from the simple past, often called the
SUBJUNCTIVE II (because the form is based on the second
principal part of the verb). The other, less common type
of subjunctive is discussed in the section *What is Meant by
Direct and Indirect Discourse?*, p. 157.

The subjunctive II form derived from the simple past
form of the indicative has a present and a past tense.

PRESENT SUBJUNCTIVE—The present subjunctive II uses the
stem of indicative past tense of the verb + subjunctive
endings.

For regular verbs, the indicative past and the subjunctive
II forms are identical:

INFINITIVE: sagen *(to say)*
PAST TENSE INDICATIVE: sagte *(I said)*
PAST STEM: sagt-

Er **sagte**...   Wenn er **sagte**...
indicative past   subjunctive II
He said...   *If he were to say*...

Here is an example of the present subjunctive II forms of
an irregular verb:

INFINITIVE: gehen *(to go)* [80]
PAST TENSE INDICATIVE: ging
PAST STEM: ging-

ich	ginge
du	gingest
er, sie, es	ginge
wir	gingen
ihr	ginget
sie, Sie	gingen

PAST SUBJUNCTIVE—The past subjunctive is formed with the auxiliary verb **haben** *(to have)* or **sein** *(to be)* in the sub- [90] junctive + the past participle of the main verb.

Ich **hätte gesagt**...
└─────┬─────┘
past subjunctive

If I had said...

Wir **wären gekommen**...
└─────┬─────┘
past subjunctive

If we had come...

Your textbook will give you a detailed explanation of all the subjunctive II forms including the verb forms that are [100] exceptions.

──────── **USAGE OF THE SUBJUNCTIVE II** ────────

The subjunctive II is commonly used in three kinds of sentences.

- expressions **CONTRARY-TO-FACT**—Unlike English where the subjunctive is only used in the *if*-clause and the verb in the result clause uses *would* + infinitive, in German, the subjunctive II is used in both the *if*-clause and in the result clause. [110]

  *If she **were** here, I **would be** happy.*
       │   │
  subjunctive   *would* + infinitive

  Wenn sie hier **wäre**, dann **wäre** ich glücklich.
              │   │
        subjunctive   subjunctive

- expressions of wishes—Unlike English where the subjunctive is only used in the conclusion of the wish-statement, in German, the subjunctive II is used in both the wish-statement and in the conclusion.

  *I **wish** she **were** here!* [120]
     │   │
  indicative   subjunctive

Ich **wünschte,** sie **wäre** doch hier!
subjunctive   subjunctive

I wish I were in Europe now!
indicative subjunctive
Ich **wünschte,** ich **wäre** jetzt in Europa!
subjunctive   subjunctive

- polite requests—Where English uses the construction *would* or *could* + the infinitive to make polite requests, German uses the verbs **können** *(to be able to)* and **werden** *(to become)* in the subjunctive II + the infinitive.

  Could you do me a favor?
  could infinitive
  Könntest du mir einen Gefallen **tun?**
  subjunctive   infinitive

  Would you please open the door?
  would   infinitive
  Würden Sie bitte die Tür **aufmachen?**
  subjunctive   infinitive

─────── **THE WÜRDE-CONSTRUCTION** ───────

In spoken German, the subjunctive II forms of the main verb are often replaced with the present subjunctive II form of **werden** *(to become)* + the infinitive of the main verb.

ich	**würde** gehen
du	**würdest** gehen
er, sie, es	**würde** gehen
wir	**würden** gehen
ihr	**würdet** gehen
sie, Sie	**würden** gehen

The structure of German sentences using the **würde**-construction is similar to the English structure using *would* + the infinitive of the main verb.

Ich **würde gehen,** wenn ich Zeit hätte.
I would go if I had time.

Sie **würden** dich **einladen,** wenn sie könnten.
They would invite you if they could.

Your textbook will explain when you should use the **würde**-construction and when you must use the subjunctive II forms.

— *REVIEW* —

Indicate whether each of the following statements is a statement of fact in the indicative (I) or a contrary-to-fact statement in the subjunctive (S).

1. West Germany is approximately the size of Oregon. I S

2. I wish I were finished already. I S

3. If I had wings, I would fly away. I S

4. Since things are going smoothly,
   we will be done soon. I S

5. If they had come earlier,
   we could have gone for a walk. I S

CHAPTER

44

WHAT IS MEANT BY ACTIVE
AND PASSIVE VOICE?

¹ VOICE in the grammatical sense refers to the relationship between the verb and its subject. There are two voices, the ACTIVE VOICE and the PASSIVE VOICE.

ACTIVE VOICE—A sentence is said to be in the active voice when the subject is the performer of the action of the verb. In this instance, the verb is called an ACTIVE VERB.

> The teacher prepares the exam.
>   S   V   DO

¹⁰
> Paul ate an apple.
>   S V   DO

> Lightning has struck the tree.
>   S   V   DO

In these examples the subject (S) performs the action of the verb (V) and the direct object (DO) is the receiver of the action (see *What is a Subject?*, p. 36 and *What are Objects?*, p. 52).

PASSIVE VOICE—A sentence is said to be in the passive voice when the subject receives the action of the verb. In this ²⁰ instance, the verb is called a PASSIVE VERB.

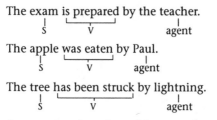

> The exam is prepared by the teacher.
>   S   V   agent

> The apple was eaten by Paul.
>   S   V   agent

> The tree has been struck by lightning.
>   S   V   agent

In these examples, the subject receives the action of the ³⁰ verb. The performer of the action, if it is mentioned, is introduced by the word "by" and is called the AGENT.

IN ENGLISH ─────────────────────────

The passive voice is expressed by the verb *to be* conjugated in the appropriate tense + the past participle of the main verb (see *What is a Participle?*, p. 89). The tense of the passive sentence is indicated by the tense of the verb *to be*.

The exam *is prepared* by the teacher.
|
present

The exam ***was** prepared* by the teacher.   40
|
past

The exam ***will be** prepared* by the teacher.
|____|
future

In English only transitive verbs (verbs that can have a direct object, see p. 52) can be used in the passive voice.

——————— MAKING AN ACTIVE SENTENCE PASSIVE ———————

The steps to change an active sentence into a passive one are as follows.   50

1. The direct object of the active sentence becomes the subject of the passive sentence.

   ACTIVE   The mechanic is repairing *the car.*
   |
   direct object

   PASSIVE   *The car* is repaired by the mechanic.
   |
   subject

2. The tense of the verb of the active sentence is reflected in the tense of the verb *to be* in the passive sentence.   60

   ACTIVE   The mechanic *repairs* the car.
   |
   present

   PASSIVE   The car *is* repaired by the mechanic.
   |
   present

   ACTIVE   The mechanic *has repaired* the car.
   |____|
   present perfect

   PASSIVE   The car *has been* repaired by the mechanic.
   |____|
   present perfect
                                                                      70

3. The subject of the active sentence becomes the agent of the passive sentence or the agent is omitted.

   ACTIVE   *The mechanic* is repairing the car.
   |
   subject

   PASSIVE   The car is being repaired *by the mechanic.*
   |
   agent

   The car is being repaired.
   |
   no agent

IN GERMAN

The passive voice is formed by the verb **werden** *(to become)* conjugated in the appropriate tense + the past participle of the main verb. The form of **werden** must agree in number with the new subject.

The tense of passive sentences is indicated by the tense of the verb **werden**.

> Der Roman **wird** gelesen.
> |
> present
> *The novel **is being** read.*

> Der Roman **wurde** gelesen.
> |
> simple past
> *The novel **was (being)** read.*

> Der Roman **wird** gelesen **werden**.
> |_____|
> future
> *The novel **will be** read.*

> Der Roman **ist** gelesen **worden**.
> |_____|
> perfect
> *The novel **was (has been)** read.*

> Der Roman **war** gelesen **worden**.
> |_____|
> pluperfect
> *The novel **had been** read.*

As you can see in the last two examples, the **ge-** of **geworden** (the past participle of **werden**) is dropped and the form **worden** is used in the passive perfect and pluperfect tenses instead.

—————— Making an active sentence passive ——————

To change an active sentence into passive in German, you can follow the same steps as for English (see p. 153). However, you will also have to change the case of the words to reflect their function in the passive sentence. The subject will always be in the nominative case, but the agent, if it is mentioned, is expressed differently depending on whether it refers to a person or not.

SUBJECT—The accusative object of an active sentence becomes the nominative subject of the passive sentence.

> ACTIVE   *The woman reads **the novel**.*
> Die Frau liest **den Roman**.
> |
> accusative

PASSIVE *The novel is read by the woman.*
Der Ro<u>m</u>an wird von der Frau gelesen.
nominative

ACTIVE *Ilse sings such songs.*
Ilse singt **solche Lieder.**
accusative

130

PASSIVE ***Such songs** are sung by Ilse.*
Solche Lie<u>d</u>er werden von Ilse gesungen.
nominative

AGENT IS A PERSON—If the nominative subject of an active sentence is a person, it is expressed by **von** + dative object.

ACTIVE ***Many people** heard the speech.*
Viele Leu<u>t</u>e hörten die Rede.
nominative

140

PASSIVE *The speech was heard **by many people**.*
Die Rede wurde **von vielen Leuten** gehört.
dative

AGENT IS NOT A PERSON—If the nominative subject of an active sentence is not a person, it is expressed by **durch** + accusative object.

ACTIVE ***Fire** has destroyed the building.*
Feu<u>e</u>r hat das Gebäude zerstört.
nominative

150

PASSIVE *The building was destroyed **by the fire**.*
Das Gebäude ist **durch das Feuer** zerstört worden.
accusative

────────── **IMPERSONAL PASSIVES** ──────────

Unlike English, German sometimes uses intransitive verbs (verbs that cannot have a direct object) in the passive voice. Such constructions are called **IMPERSONAL PASSIVES**, because the verb expresses an activity with no reference to a personal subject.

160

Some intransitive verbs can be followed by a dative object. If you change a sentence that has only a dative object from active to passive, the object remains in the dative case instead of becoming the subject of the passive sentence.

ACTIVE   Man dankt **ihm**.
|
dative object
*One thanks **him**.*

PASSIVE   **Ihm** wird gedankt.
|
dative subject
He is thanked.

ACTIVE   Sie glaubten **den Kindern** nicht.
|
dative object
*They didn't believe **the children**.*

PASSIVE   **Den Kindern** wurde nicht geglaubt.
|
dative subject
***The children** were not believed.*

Note that many impersonal passives in German cannot be translated word-for-word into English.

Your textbook will show you several alternatives to the passive construction in German.

— REVIEW —

I. Underline the subject in the following sentences.
- Circle the performer of the action.
- Identify each sentence as active (A) or passive (P).

1. The cow jumped over the moon.   A   P

2. The game was cut short by rain.   A   P

3. They camped by the river.   A   P

4. This film will be enjoyed by everyone.   A   P

II. Underline the verb in the following sentences.
- Identify the tense of each sentences: past (PA), present (P), future (F).
- Keeping the same tense, rewrite the sentence in the passive voice on the line provided.

1. The parents dropped off the children.   PA   P   F

_____

2. Work crews are clearing the road.   PA   P   F

_____

3. People all over the world will see this program.   PA   P   F

_____

WHAT IS MEANT BY DIRECT AND INDIRECT DISCOURSE?

In **DIRECT DISCOURSE** a statement is made directly
between a speaker and a listener.
Direct discourse is usually
set in quotation marks.

Mary said, "I am going to Berlin."
John asked, "What will you do in Berlin?"

In **INDIRECT DISCOURSE** (also called **REPORTED
DISCOURSE**) another person's statement
is transmited without quoting
their words directly.

Mary said she was going to Berlin.
John asked what would I do in Berlin.

Notice that while indirect discourse reproduces the substance of the message, it cannot reproduce the statement word-for-word.

IN ENGLISH

When direct discourse is changed to indirect discourse some words (such as pronouns, possessive adjectives) must be changed to reflect the change of speaker. There is also a shift in tense.

DIRECT DISCOURSE	Mary said, "**I am going** to Berlin."
	PRONOUNS: I → she
	TENSE: am going (present) → was going (past)
INDIRECT DISCOURSE	Mary said **she was going** to Berlin.
DIRECT DISCOURSE	Mary said, "**I was** in Berlin with **my** sister."
	PRONOUNS: I → she
	POSSESSIVE ADJECTIVE: my → her
	TENSE: was (past) → had been (past perfect)
INDIRECT DISCOURSE	Mary said **she had been** in Berlin with **her** sister.

IN GERMAN

As in English, when direct discourse is changed to indirect discourse the pronouns used in the original statement are changed. Unlike English where there is only a shift in tense, in German there is a shift in mood. In direct discourse the verb is in the indicative, in indirect discourse the verb is in a form of the subjunctive called the SUBJUNCTIVE OF INDIRECT DISCOURSE or SUBJUNCTIVE I (because the form is based on the first principal part of the verb).

Let us look at how the subjunctive I is formed to express indirect discourse in the present and past tenses.

PRESENT SUBJUNCTIVE—The present subjunctive I uses the stem of the infinitive + the subjunctive endings.

DIRECT DISCOURSE   Mary sagte, "Ich **fahre** nach Berlin."

present indicative

Mary said, "I am going to Berlin."

INDIRECT DISCOURSE   Mary sagte, sie **fahre** nach Berlin.

subjunctive I present

Mary said she was going to Berlin.

PAST SUBJUNCTIVE—The past tense subjunctive I uses the subjunctive I form of the helping verb **haben** *(to have)* or **sein** *(to be)* + the past participle of the main verb.

DIRECT DISCOURSE   Mary sagte, "Ich **war** in Berlin."

simple past indicative

Mary said, "I was in Berlin."

INDIRECT DISCOURSE   Mary sagte, sie **sei** in Berlin **gewesen**.

subjunctive I past

Mary said she had been in Berlin.

In conversation, the subjunctive II (see p. 149) is often used for indirect discourse. Your German textbook will explain in greater detail the formation and use of the indirect discourse subjunctive.

— REVIEW —

Underline the verbs in the quotations below.
- Indicate whether the verb describes an action in the present (P) or in the past (PA).
- Box in any pronouns or possessive adjectives within the quotation that will change when these sentences are in indirect discourse.
- Rewrite these direct discourse sentences as indirect discourse.

1. She asked, "How is the weather?"   P   PA

   She asked _____

2. They shouted, "We found the trail."   P   PA

   They shouted that _____

3. He announced, "I just got my driver's license."   P   PA

   He announced that _____

4. Libby said, "I'm coming."   P   PA

   Libby said that _____

5. Tony called out, "I'm done."   P   PA

   Tony called out that _____

1. What is a Noun? 1. Katie, teacher, questions, Europe
2. Mrs. Schneider, students, patience 3. curiosity, part, learning 4. Katie, classmates, stories, Berlin, capital, Germany
5. class, exhibit, settlers
2. What is Meant by Gender? 1. M 2. N 3. F 4. M 5. F
3. What is Meant by Number? I. 1. plural 2. singular
3. singular 4. plural 5. singular II. 1. ö + -er 2. ü + -e 3. -er
4. -nen 5. -s
4. What are Articles? 1. das 2. ein 3. eine 4. das 5. ein
6. die 7. der
5. What is a Pronoun? The antecedent is between parentheses: 1. she (Brooke) 2. they (Molly and Stan) 3. it (chair)
4. himself (Jim) 5. her (Helga)
7. What is a Verb? 1. meet 2. eat 3. stayed, expected
4. took, finished, went 5. felt, talked
8. What is the Infinitive? 1. teach 2. be 3. have 4. leave
5. swim
9. What are Prefixes and Suffixes? I. 1. de- 2. en- 3. mis-
II. 1. -ency 2. -ful 3. -less
12. What is a Subject Pronoun? 1. Q:Who goes?
A: I (Singular) 2. Q: Who are? A: My brother and sister
(Plural) 3. Q: Who doesn't work? A: They (Plural) 4. Q: Who
has to work? A: I (Singular)
13. What is a Predicate Noun? The subject is between
parentheses: 1. news (letter) 2. doctor (Carol) 3. tourists
(they) 4. musician (Dan) 5. place (pool)
14. What is a Verb Conjugation? I. 1. denk- 2. renn-
3. arbeit- 4. wander- 5. reis- II. STEM: geh-; gehe, gehst,
geht, gehen, geht, gehen
15. What is a Sentence? I. 1. to do your best (IP) 2. Before
the play (PrP) 3. at the last minute (PP) 4. to start early (IP),
5. organizing her room (PP) II. 1. While you were out
2. Although we were tired 3. that they were ready 4. if you
want to go with us 5. After the sun set III. 1. snowed
2. looked 3. goes 4. have 5. were
16. What are Objects? 1. A: my homework (DO) 2. A: a
postcard (DO) A: her friend (IO) 3. A: the books (OP) A: a
credit card (OP)
17. What are Direct and Indirect Object Pronouns?
1. 2nd, singular, dative 2. 3rd, masculine, singular, accusative
3. 3rd, feminine, singular

18. What is the Possessive? I. The possessor is in italics: 1. the motors of the *cars* 2. the end of the *year* 3. the works of *Bachmann*

19. What are the Principal Parts of a Verb? 1. W 2. S 3. S 4. W 5. S

21. What is Meant by Mood? 1. indicative 2. subjunctive 3. imperative 4. indicative 5. imperative

22. What is the Imperative? 1. du 2. wir 3. ihr 4. Sie 5. du

23. What are Auxiliary Verbs? The auxiliary verbs and modals are in parentheses; the English auxiliaries that will not be expressed are in italics; the verbs that will be expressed in German are outside the parentheses: 1. (*are* working) working 2. (can go) can go 3. (*do* have) have 4. (*has* waited) waited 5. (*will* arrive) arrive

24. What is the Present Tense? 1. do play 2. plays 3. is playing 4. are playing 5. play

25. What is the Past Tense? I. 1. went (SP) 2. has visited (PP) 3. was (SP) 4. travelled (SP) 5. have shown (PP)

26. What are the Perfect Tenses? 1. had gone (PP) 2. hasn't left (P) 3. will have graduated (FP) 4. have seen (P)

27. What is the Future Tense? 1. are going → present 2. will go → future 3. shall return → future 4. am flying → present 5. '11 be → future

28. What is a Participle? I. 1. watching (P) 2. gone (PP) 3. broken (PP) 4. studying (P)

29. What is an Interrogative Pronoun? 1. who, person, subject → **wer** 2. what, thing, direct object → **was** 3. whose, person (or thing), possessive → **wessen** 4. who (for whom), person, object of preposition → **wen**

30. What is a Possessive Pronoun? 1. yours 2. ours 3. hers 4. his 5. mine

32. What is a Possessive Adjective? I. The possessive adjective is in italics: 1. *their* exams 2. *her* coat, *her* scarf 3. *his* comb, *his* pocket

33. What is a Demonstrative Adjective? The modified noun is in parentheses: 1. every (room) 2. this (house) 3. all (houses) 4. these (windows) 5. those (closets)

34. What is an Interrogative Adjective? I. The interrogative adjective is in italics: 1. *what* newspaper 2. *which* record 3. *what* homework 4. *which* hotel 5. *which* game II. 1. About which topic did you write? 2. To which people did you talk?

35. What is a Descriptive Adjective? I. The noun or pronoun described is between parentheses: 1. red (door) AE 2. fresh (juice) AD 3. old (shoes) NA 4. large (pizza) AD, 5. friendly (face) AE

36. What is Meant by Comparison of Adjectives? 1. The teacher is older than the students. 2. This student is as intelligent as that one. 3. Kathy is less tall than Molly. 4. This movie is the best this season. 5. Today is the hottest day on record.

37. What are Reflexive Pronouns and Verbs? I. 1. yourself 2. ourselves 3. himself 4. herself 5. myself 6. yourselves II. mich, dich, sich, uns, euch, sich

38. What is an Adverb? The word modified is after the comma: 1. early, arrived 2. too, tired 3. really, quickly, learned 4. here, stayed 5. very, well, speaks

39. What is a Preposition? I. 1. behind 2. under 3. at, in 4. on, around II. 1. I can't tell about what they're laughing. 2. For whom are you doing that?

40. What are Object of Preposition Pronouns? Nouns referring to persons are in italics: 1. *Greg*, preposition + pronoun 2. present, da-compound 3. *Emily*, preposition + pronoun 4. vacation, da-compound

41. What is a Conjunction? I. 1. unless 2. because 3. but II.: 1. since 2. since 3. before 4. before

42. What is a Relative Pronoun? The antecedent is in italics: I. 1. *letter*, that → DO 2. *people*,who → S 3. *woman*, whom → DO 4. *book*, whose → PM 5. *student*, whom → OP

43. What is the Subjunctive? 1. I 2. S 3. S 4. I 5. S

44. What is Meant by Active and Passive Voice? I. The subject is followed by the performer of the action in italics: 1. cow, *cow* → A 2. game, *rain* → P 3. they, *they* → A 4. film, *everyone* → P II. 1. dropped (PA) → The children were dropped off by the parents. 2. are clearing (P) → The road is being cleared by work crews. 3. will see (F) → This program will be seen by people all over the world.

45. What is Meant by Direct and Indirect Discourse? 1. "How is the weather?" 2. "We have found the trail." 3. "I'm coming."